Advance Praise for *While Jesus Weeps*

"Saniel Bonder's *While Jesus Weeps* has had a lasting and profound effect on my life. From a spiritual point of view, my late teenage years – in the late 60s and early 70s – were filled with an almost unbelievable commitment and dedication toward finding the profound spiritual oneness in all things. It was a spiritual renaissance in America and we had no tradition to look to for guidance. Saniel's book – which I heard him read aloud at a yoga retreat in 1972 – spoke to so much of my mind's confusion. The clarity and sincerity as well as the obviously mature and serious thought that was evident in his work pointed to a possible future for me in which these struggles had a place in real adult life and actually had been around on the Earth for a long time. *While Jesus Weeps* gave me hope and insight into what has turned out to be my own and humanity's major struggle – to integrate real spiritual truths into our human existence in the world."

– Geoffrey Gordon, composer and percussionist

"I have followed Saniel Bonder's career since he first enrolled at Webb School in Tennessee, where I was then headmaster. A warm and mutually supportive relationship between us has existed over the years. While he was still a student at Harvard, Saniel shared with me the original manuscript of *While Jesus Weeps*.

"A lifelong Christian, I was deeply moved by the insight shown by this young man. This is a living expression of what might well have taken place that fatal night. This makes you think."

– Henry Whiteside, retired business executive and educator

While Jesus Weeps

#_____ of 750

Special Prepublication Edition

Also by Saniel Bonder

Waking Down: Beyond Hypermasculine Dharmas – A Breakthrough Way of Self-Realization in the Sanctuary of Mutuality

The White-Hot Yoga of the Heart: Divinely Human Self-Realization and Sacred Marriage – Especially for "Westerners"

The Perpetual Cosmic Out-of-Court Payoff Machine: Selected Essays on Living with Whole-Being Integrity

While Jesus Weeps

Conversations in the Garden of Gethsemane

A Novel

by Saniel Bonder

Mt. Tam Awakenings, Inc.

Library of Congress Cataloging-in-Publication Data

Bonder, Saniel
While Jesus weeps: conversations in the garden of gethsemane
/ Saniel Bonder. — Special prepublication ed.

ISBN 0-966-2304-1-8
Saniel Bonder — Fiction/Spirituality

Mt. Tam Awakenings, Inc., San Anselmo, California

Printed in the United States of America

2 4 6 8 9 7 5 3

SPECIAL PREPUBLICATION EDITION

Cover design by Linda Groves
Cover art by Ted Strauss
This book is set in Palatino type.

For everyone who yearns to dwell in the sacred mystery of our existence, and especially those who wonder what it might have been like to live in Jesus's time, to meet him in the flesh, and to consecrate one's life to his ministry – on his own terms.

With special gratitude to Dale Schmidt, Mary McClelland, Henry Whiteside, Sean Reily and Leanne Senter-Barbour, a fellow writer who prefers anonymity, and that mysterious "man in a blanket" in India, each of whom helped so much to make this book possible.

"Verily, verily, I say unto you,
except a corn of wheat fall into the
ground and die, it abideth alone;
but if it die, it bringeth forth
much fruit."

John XII.24
(King James version)

"Jesus said we must understand one another.
Jesus said we must understand one another.
Jesus said we must understand one another.
Jesus said we must understand
one another."

Kitaro
Dream

CONTENTS

The Characters

Peter (Simon Peter)
Andrew (Peter's brother)
James, son of Zebedee
John ("the Beloved"; James's brother)
Matthew, the former tax-gatherer
Philip
Thaddeus
Bartholomew
James, son of Alphaeus ("James Alphaeus")
Simon (the Zealot)
Thomas

First Conversation

The Apostles of Jesus are huddling in the Garden of Gethsemane, just east of the city of Jerusalem, on the night of the Last Supper. They sit in a partial clearing surrounded on three sides by trees, mostly fig and olive, and bushes. The clearing opens or faces to the north. Overhead branches cast a maze of indistinct shadows in the pale, diffuse twilight. The olive trees apparently have been picked clean, none of the figs have yet borne fruit, and none of the bushes have flowered. The trees, thick behind the men just north of the clearing, thin out but do not entirely yield to the bushes around and among them, with more trees to the east and the west.

A few rocks and boulders dot the clearing, all large enough to sit on, including one huge mass sloping up and forward from the back of the central area to the west. The landscape suggests that there is higher, rocky ground behind the Apostles and their clearing, but no distinct rise is visible through and beyond the trees. In the open space there is no grass. A path, discernible through the dust, disappears into the trees at the left and to the rear, in a southeasterly direction. Two swords lean against a tree on the western edge of the area, also to the rear. They are out of the way but plainly visible from all sides.

The Apostles pull their shawls and cloaks tight against the still wintry chill. Resting under the trees and around the clearing, they form a vague crescent. Some are slumped on the ground, some pace about slowly, some sit on rocks and fidget, some pray for a few moments, fitfully. All their expressions indicate discomfort and tension. Not a word is spoken for some time.

Thomas, thin-bearded and wiry, is sprawled in the dust near the trees in the left central background of the clearing. He suddenly clutches at his heart and moans aloud.

Andrew, older and heavier, has been squirming about on a rock nearby. Roused, he whispers, "What is it, Thomas?"

Thomas shakes his head and grimaces. "That meal . . . "

Several of the others laugh quietly. They're nervous, reluctant to make any sound.

Andrew presses his own belly. "Oh . . . I'm not feeling too well myself."

For a few moments there is silence. James, tall and thin, seated on a rock between Thomas and Andrew, shakes his head from side to side, pondering. When he speaks, it is from deep preoccupation with his thoughts, as if the last words had only just been uttered. "I don't imagine any of us are feeling very good after that meal." He tries to smother a belch.

Philip is leaning against a tree off to the far right. "No. That lamb was almost raw," he says, his voice low but harsh.

"Bloody, too," Thomas adds. Then, "Innkeeper ought to be stoned."

Andrew glances at him. "Well . . . you're probably right. And I drank too much."

Matthew, a gray and portly man, visibly the oldest among them, is crouched on a boulder near the center of the group. "Too much, too fast," he mutters. "And the bread was not only unleavened . . . it was unbaked!"

James, still lost in thought, looks up, puzzled. His voice is louder than he realizes: "I didn't think the food was all *that* bad . . . I was referring to the things he said. *That's* what's hard for me to digest."

Matthew frowns, pressing his belly. "Yes. He really let us have it tonight."

"What terrible things," Andrew says. "I don't know why all that has to be."

Matthew is shaking his head. "On such a holy, festive night, too. Said we were freed slaves. . . . Hm." He puts his head in his hands.

Philip looks at Matthew and Andrew with a smile, and snorts, but doesn't speak. James either doesn't hear Philip, or ignores him. "All that about eating his flesh and blood. About his 'hour' coming soon, and his being betrayed by one . . . of us. Making us carry those swords with us." He glances at the others, then looks down.

Sitting on the ground to the left, within the crescent formed by the others, Thaddeus was trying to pray. For the last few moments he has been looking at each speaker and listening, biting his lip. He says, too loud,

"I'm – I'm really afraid about what he said is going to happen tonight."

No one replies. The only sound is Peter's footsteps. A formidable man, of medium height but built like a wrestler, he has also been praying, but is now pacing about near the center of the clearing. He stops. There is a hush.

"Then *pray*, Thaddeus," Peter says, with a harsh whisper. "He told us to pray!"

Thomas smiles. "Then what are you doing walking around and talking, Simon Peter?"

Matthew sighs. "Brothers . . . not tonight. Please."

Andrew looks up at his sibling. "Peter, we must speak of these things."

Bartholomew is perhaps the youngest among them, with no beard and a softness to his features. He is sitting on the ground near the low end of the large boulder, to the right, and is, now, one of the last to open his eyes from prayer. "But the Master just now told us to *pray*, Andrew. That we might be spared the test!" His words are muted and shrill. "He's praying now, himself, up on that hill" – he points to the rear – "what if he knew we were down here talking?"

No one replies. Peter sits down on the base of the large boulder, near the center.

"He's right, brothers," Peter says, softly. "Jesus has commanded us to pray. We must pray. Anything else and . . . we'd betray his trust."

James Alphaeus, small, tight-faced, has been kneeling just outside the crescent of the others, to the left, on the eastern border of the clearing. Still scowling, not moving or even opening his eyes from his attitude of prayer, he says, "And he would condemn us to the pit!"

No one speaks. Most close their eyes and begin silent prayer again. But only a few of them relax into it; the others, agitated, fidget, frown, or sigh.

Finally Thaddeus leaps up with an outcry: "It's no use!" He looks around at the others, flushing. "I can't do it. I don't want to talk, but I can't pray either, and I'll go mad thinking about it all." He closes his eyes. "I don't even want to think about it – but we *must* speak about what's happening with him, and us!"

Everyone else, except Bartholomew, Peter, and James Alphaeus, soon opens his eyes. For a moment no one makes another sound. The other Simon, the Zealot, a huge, brooding man with an immense face, has been sitting off to the right side, gazing into the last light of the sunset. Now he too turns to listen.

Andrew nods his head. "Yes, brothers, let's speak of these things. We've been doing nothing but proclaiming the Gospel and walking, walking, walking for so long."

Matthew belches. "But what is there to say?"

"Well," James ventures, "at least we could try to remember exactly what he said." He shakes his head and sighs. "All this dread and apocalypse these last few

days. And now he says it's one of *us* who'll betray him
. . . *how* did he say that? Anyone remember?"

Andrew nods again. "He said. . . . " He pauses,
waiting for the others' full attention. "He said, 'I'll tell
you this, one of you will betray me – one who is eating
with me.'"

"There was no one eating with him but us,"
Philip says.

Bartholomew's eyes are closed; he talks from his
prayers. "Oh, God. Oh, Lord." He opens his eyes and
looks around at some of the others, his gaze vacant, as if
not recognizing them.

All fall silent. Philip looks around at the circle of
men with a glint in his eye. When he speaks, his tone is
still flat, matter of fact. "And then every single one of us
asked, 'Not *I*, Lord?' And he said, 'It is one of the Twelve
who is dipping into the same bowl with me.'"

Thomas sits bolt upright. "Did anybody *not* dip
into the bowl?"

James clucks at him. "Thomas!"

"No, I mean it," Thomas snaps. "I'm in this as
much as you are."

"Of course everyone dipped into the bowl," James
says. "It was the Seder, the Passover meal."

"Mm," Thomas says. "I forgot." He becomes
thoughtful.

Silence again. Philip eyes them all. He is still standing at a slight distance from most of them. Now he walks

closer. "Does anybody remember what he said . . . about the betrayer?"

Simon nods once, with power. "He said, 'The Son of Man is going the way appointed for him in Scripture, but alas for the man by whom the Son of Man is betrayed. It would be better for that man if he had never been born.'" Simon looks away again, a curl to his lips.

Thomas rolls his eyes. "Thank you, Simon. Thank you very much."

Once again, a hush. Uncomfortable on his rock, James shifts his gaunt form. "And we all sat there like grains of wheat under a grindstone. But what was it Peter and John were whispering to him? John?"

John has been sitting on the far right, under the shadows of a leafless tree, looking away all along. Now he turns toward his brother and shrugs.

"Nothing important."

Peter sighs aloud. He makes a fist of one of his just-clasped hands and lightly strikes the heel of that hand in his other palm. "I asked John to ask him who it was he meant. What did he whisper back to you, John?"

Bartholomew's eyes are wide. *"John?"*

John looks at the others one by one. His gaze is so direct that each of them soon looks aside. He turns away again. There is a long pause. No one moves or looks up, but they are all listening. John lowers his head and speaks, his voice so quiet that some of them lift their ears toward him. "He said he wouldn't tell me."

"Hm," James murmurs. "Might have known he'd say that." He raises his brows and shakes his head, then cranes his neck and head toward the earth. "Hm. Hm. Hm."

Peter opens his mouth, as if about to speak, but remains silent. Soon he closes his eyes and clasps his hands, returning to silent prayer. With a sour grin on his face, Thomas follows Peter's movements, then glances at some of the others. "Well," he says. "Here we all are."

No one responds. Matthew presses his hand deep into his abdomen and grimaces.

Thomas, still looking around at them, sets his jaw. "All right!" His eyes are flashing. "Someone's got to confess. Right now!"

Bartholomew whirls toward him. "Thomas, how can you joke like this, when we're all about to break in half?"

"Why?" Thomas is eyeing Bartholomew.

"Why what?"

Thomas darts around the boulder and stands behind Bartholomew. "Why are you about to break in half?"

Bartholomew shifts, trying to turn to face Thomas. "What? I mean . . . don't all of us feel wrenched apart? I'm terrified. Aren't you?"

Thomas leans closer. "Why are *you* terrified, Bartholomew?"

Andrew turns toward Thomas. "Bartholomew

is anguished enough, Thomas. Why are you tormenting him?"

Thomas's eyes do not leave Bartholomew's face.
"Maybe he's tormented because he's planning to
betray Jesus."

Andrew snorts and laughs.

"One of us has to do it!" Thomas says.

Like lightning, Philip is standing in front of
Bartholomew, leaning over him to grasp Thomas's cloak.
"And if it's someone else, then it's not you, right?"

"No! – Yes!" Thomas yanks his shoulder from
Philip's hand. "Look: we all want to know who the
betrayer is. Come, admit it! And if we can find him –
and he's right here, isn't he? – then maybe we can stop
him from betraying the Master. Couldn't we?"

James Alphaeus still has not opened his eyes from
prayer. "The Lord has to be betrayed. Scripture says so."

Thomas twists his lips to one side of his face. "Oh.
Well, then at least we can get it straight for ourselves. So
if Bartholomew is 'wrenched apart,' I want to know why."

Philip is still eyeing him. "But why should the
betrayer make himself conspicuous? If I were him,
I'd keep my mouth shut and follow along with everyone else."

There are nods and mumbles of agreement – then
silence. For a moment none of them looks into anyone
else's eyes. Fingering his beard, then running his hand
through his thinning hair, Matthew scans the group.

"Look at us!" he whispers. "Like animals at each other's throats."

Andrew nods. "You're right. Just tonight Jesus commanded us to love one another, and here we are spitting like snakes."

"Well," Thomas says, "He told us to be wary as serpents – "

"And innocent as doves," James cuts in. "It's true, trying to find the betrayer will only bring hatred and distrust among us. We're all in this garden together."

"Yes," Matthew affirms. He huddles his shawl tighter around his shoulders.

The garden is quiet. There is no breeze, no sound but that of their own bodies as they shift and squirm.

Andrew suddenly looks up and all around. "Where's Judas?" He leaps to his feet. *"Where's Judas?"*

They all look at one another, peering through the clearing and into the trees.

"Judas," Bartholomew muses. "He left during supper, remember?"

Philip lets out a low hiss, then cuts it short. "And he hasn't returned!"

"So we're not 'all in this garden together,'" James says.

Thomas remembers more. "Of course! The Master handed him a piece of bread and spoke to him, and quick as a bat he was gone!"

Philip is striding about. "What did the

Master say to him?"

Thomas raises his eyebrows and shrugs.

Philip turns sharply. "Peter was nearby, Peter?" Peter does not stir from prayer. "Didn't anybody hear? No one?"

Andrew's eyes are shut tight. "I think I heard him. He said, 'Do what you have to do.'"

Several shout at once, "Yes! Of course!"

They look at one another, wide-eyed, then away. After a pause, James clears his throat. "That's odd. We all remember it now. How could we all have forgotten that – 'do what you have to do.'"

"It was right after Jesus talked about the betrayer," Matthew says. "But what he said to Judas seemed unimportant, he didn't weigh his words. We probably all thought Judas had to run an errand, because he keeps the purse."

"Hah!" Thomas laughs. "'Run an errand.'"

Philip breaks a small branch off a tree. "Wait. So Judas isn't here. Does that make him the betrayer? Maybe he *is* running an errand. Maybe he got sick and had to retch. It still might be one of us."

"Maybe," James says, "but whatever is going to happen, it's going to start soon. And Judas did leave right after this betrayal affair came up."

He swings around to face his brother. "John? Are you sure Jesus didn't say anything else to you? Didn't hint, or wink, or gesture?"

John turns toward James without expression. "No. He didn't."

Thomas now strides about in front of them all. "But how blatant do you want him to get? He tells John, no, I won't say who my betrayer is; then out of nowhere he turns to Judas and says, 'Do what you have to do,' and Judas ups and disappears. What more do you want?"

Andrew looks all around beyond the clearing. "Where *is* Judas?"

Bartholomew's eyes are wide again. "He must be out arranging our Lord's betrayal. . . . "

"Wait, wait, wait," Matthew says. "He didn't *say* Judas is his betrayer, so it's wrong for us to assume it."

"What has he ever *said* outright?" Philip gesticulates. "He's always talking in figures of speech, acting out prophecies. This whole mission is some huge parable – and you expect him to say outright, 'Judas here is going to betray me now'? And maybe have Judas bow before us?"

Thomas is still pacing, his eyes flashing. "Hold on, Philip. Let's not avoid looking at this. Anyone notice what Judas has been like lately?"

Andrew eyes him. "Why, you were his bosom friend, Thomas."

"No, I wasn't," Thomas says.

"Certainly you were, Thomas!" James tries to rise, but loses his balance and almost falls. He steadies himself. Then he and Philip move to approach Thomas.

"You and Judas were always sticking together, and making jokes."

Thomas regards James. His eyes betray no feeling. "But I've hardly spoken with him in the last month."

"What are you up to here, Thomas?" Philip growls. "Why not?"

Thomas slides down onto a rock to his right. "Well, he . . . just started drawing away from me, that's all. He wouldn't talk the way we used to."

Philip is now standing over him. "What did you used to talk about?"

"Just this and that," Thomas says, looking aside. "We'd discuss whatever was happening. We'd – just talk."

James leans over to stare him in the face. "And Judas suddenly drew away from your 'just talks'?"

Thomas nods.

Philip snorts again. "I don't know whether to believe you, Thomas. But if that's true, if he just didn't want to talk any more . . . I wonder why." He turns to James. "Do you think maybe he'd already begun plotting?"

"Maybe," James says. "It doesn't look as though we can be sure."

Matthew sits up straight, frowning. "But wait, don't you remember? It was just around a month ago that Judas suddenly seemed to fall in love with Jesus, or something."

"What?" Philip and James shout.

"I remember," Andrew says. "I guess it was about then, Judas was often beaming and smiling . . . but he never spoke to me so I don't really know."

"Me either," Bartholomew adds. "How'd you know that, Matthew? I didn't know you were close with him."

Matthew looks about at the others, blinking. "I – I thought it was common knowledge – "

Philip moves in front of Matthew and stands over him. "Come now, Matthew! What did Judas tell you, and where, and when?"

"N – *nothing*, really," Matthew blurts out.

Philip's voice is like ice. "Come clean, you old thief!"

Matthew heaves a sigh. "All right, all right. Get away, Philip. This won't make things any easier, I assure you.

"Shortly after this change began coming over him, Judas took me aside – I guess he knew I hadn't completely . . . well, he suggested we go into a village for a skin of wine. I saw no harm and was pleased at the chance to get to know him – he'd always seemed distant. But when we got to the inn and sat down, he looked at the wine and suddenly jumped up and said, 'No, it's not wrong, but I can't betray his trust now. He doesn't want me to, I can't!' I said what are you talking about, of course we're both sinning but let's go ahead and enjoy it as long as we're here. But he took my hand in both of his and said, 'So you see I can't, I can't betray his trust now.' And then he asked me to forgive him.

"Well, I thought he might be a little feverish – it was quite a scene, and then begging *my* forgiveness? – so I told him to do as he wished, and he thanked me, weeping, and ran out. I've hardly spoken with him since."

Philip has taken a few steps back from Matthew. He leans closer again. "Where'd he go then? Why didn't you catch him and take him back to where you were staying, if you thought he was feverish?"

Matthew shrugs.

Andrew is smiling at the older man through narrowed eyes. "Hm. We all thought you'd given up your drinking, Matthew!"

Ignoring Andrew, James pursues the investigation. "All right. It looks as though nobody but Matthew and Thomas has spoken with Judas closely in the last month or so. Anyone talk with him much before that?"

"No, James," Bartholomew says. "He was always so private. Except when he and Thomas were making jokes, and then he was always superficial or ironic or even mean."

James asks, "Did anyone notice him around the Master, just the two of them, much around that time?"

Several shake their heads.

Philip steps in again. "So all we know, according

to what Matthew says, is that not long ago Judas went through some kind of major change."

"And since then," Andrew adds, "I've sometimes seen him hanging back and smiling almost secretly. He seemed aloof, kind of haughty, though not unfriendly, not cruel. But sometimes I also caught a look of fear in his eyes – and, even sorrow."

For an instant all are still. Thomas rises and nimbly climbs to the top of the main rock mass, where he perches, sitting on his haunches. Then James speaks. "Yes, Judas has been pleasant enough lately, in my encounters with him – but there's been some kind of tightness in him, too, a hidden excitement; something's been driving him."

"We can't know anything from mere appearances!" Philip says. He pauses, then looks up at Thomas. "But we still don't know what he used to talk to Thomas *about*. We just know they talked."

James grunts agreement. "Thomas? What *did* you talk about?"

Thomas doesn't look at them. "I told you, just what Jesus was doing at the moment in our mission."

James glances at Thomas, shakes his head, and spits into the dirt. "For a brotherhood of disciples, we certainly are evading each other tonight. *How* did you talk about it? What was his attitude?"

"According to Matthew's story," Bartholomew pipes in, "he must have had some doubts back then, don't you think? And all his joking?"

Philip strides over and reaches up to poke Thomas in the chest. "Doubts, doubts! Is that what went on, the two of you grumbling and plotting together?"

"You're one to ask, Philip." Thomas looks Philip straight in the eyes. "No – that's not at all what happened. Judas did speak of his doubts, yes, but I was merely trying to help him through them. That's why we joked together, too."

"You're lying through your teeth!" Philip's voice cuts the air, a hissing whisper. "You're just trying to protect yourself and incriminate Judas!" He turns and pauses, then whirls back toward Thomas.

"Tell me, Thomas, if this isn't true: the reason you started this investigation here is because *you* were planning with Judas to betray the Master . . . but you became frightened tonight at the table – and so you hoped now to discover if anyone else was plotting, just to get yourself off the hook! Just to persuade yourself that he doesn't really know your plans, that you're not doomed! You and Judas both!"

"Wait, Philip, you're losing control." James places a hand on Philip's shoulder. "How can Thomas and Judas both be damned? The Master spoke of only one betrayer, he said he didn't mean all of us. Only one."

Philip shakes off James's hand with a violent shrug. "So what? He also said nothing's impossible with God! How do you know he won't come down from that hilltop and say, 'My disciples, the heavenly Father has just made it plain to me – you are *all* going to betray me and be sent to eternal fire!' He just told us out there on the Mount of Olives that we would *all* lose our faith. From there, who knows what will happen?"

Thomas's reply is steady and quiet. "He also said he would go on before us into Galilee after he is raised, Philip. Now I'm sure I don't understand that, but it did seem definite there would be only one betrayer."

Philip is still storming about. "'Seemed definite'! *What's definite any more?* The only thing we rely on as definite is what he says, and most of that doesn't make any sense to us." He slumps to the ground at the base of a tree. "We don't know anything for certain, except that we're sitting here in the dark waiting to see who's drawn the short straw, like slave gladiators in a Roman dungeon."

James clears his throat. "*Well*, Philip – "

"*Well* what?" Philip shouts. "Do *you* know anything about what's going to happen next?" He snorts. "*Wise* man."

Those who are not praying sit brooding in the silence. Peter comes out of prayer, followed by James Alphaeus. Peter beholds Philip with a steady, calm gaze. "Philip, it won't avail us to question or wonder about this matter. If you have faith, then you are in no danger; only pray, as the Lord said, that you might be spared the test. If you don't have faith, don't torment those who do. Their trials are severe enough at this moment."

"Perhaps you didn't hear me, Peter," Philip snarls. "*He* said we *all* – "

James Alphaeus cuts in. "Philip, you had better watch yourself! Remember his words: 'Woe to the man who is a stumbling-block for these little ones – it would be better for him if a millstone were set around his neck, and he were thrown out to sea!'"

Philip glowers at James Alphaeus, then Peter, then James, but does not speak.

James begins to stroll about.

"Listen," he says, "that's not really the point now. If a man has questions, can he throw them out of his mind? Of course not. No, the point is – "

"He *must* throw them out of his mind," Peter says.

James smiles. "Ah, Peter. We've always disagreed on this. Even before Jesus." He stops, and glances up into the trees, then back at Philip.

"All right, never mind that, just look at this, Philip: it's not all as terribly predetermined as you feel. It's just not. The whole of our people's history in covenant with God has been predicated upon man's freedom before his countenance."

Philip spits. "James, how you have persisted in pretensions to scholarship these three years mystifies me. Look at this moment. Right here, right now! Do you feel *free*? Ever since we met Jesus, we've been doing nothing but helplessly fulfilling prophecies. Our minds have been closed, so he says, not necessarily because we're idiots, but so the Word of God could be fulfilled: 'He spake, but lo, their minds were dull and gross.'

"*Lo* indeed. Please, James, don't talk to me about freedom, I have no idea what you mean." Philip looks up at James with a bitter smile, shaking his head.

James reflects for a moment, then returns to his rock on the left and sits again. "I'm not pretending to be a scholar, Philip. I am talking about how we live with God.

"I won't deny there is a certain amount of prede-termination in our being where we are and who we are at the present moment. But your fears are actually groundless if you have been just and righteous in the Law. My fears, too; I won't deny having them."

As James continues, he frequently looks at his hands, or at the ground; now and again he engages Philip's gaze. "But God has guaranteed that. Have you ever read Ezekiel? There's no way you can be condemned unless you deserve it. And even if you do, if you but turn to God and repent, you shall be redeemed. God told Ezekiel, the fathers may eat sour grapes, but the children's teeth will no longer be set on edge, as it was in the past. In the same way, you or I won't be condemned for some-one else's past evil.

"It's not as if we're drawing lots or being chosen to die at random in the dungeon by some tyrannical Centurion-God. You've been free all your life to choose good or evil; if you've chosen evil, you're now free to turn and repent. God won't break His promises to us. We always stand in His presence. You talk about this moment, but actually you're worried about what's going to happen next. We find ourselves thrown for some reason into this moment; but if we turn to God in this moment, what is there to fear in the next?" James looks away from Philip, musing. "That's why the Master told us to pray, I guess; to pray we might be spared."

Philip opens his mouth to reply, but either can't find words or chooses not to say them. He looks away sharply.

They all try to pray again. Some, like Philip, quit within instants. No one remains in prayer for more than a moment or two. Philip is waiting for James to open his eyes.

"James," he taunts, "you're able to recite marvelously from Scripture, but your words don't seem to be foremost on God's tongue these days. The Master says if we are *his* disciples and dwell in *his* revelation, 'You shall know the truth, and the truth shall set you free.' Now neither you nor I know the truth yet, so we must not be so free as you think. And the Scriptures the *Master* refers to – come, James! They're all about the terrible things Israel is going to do – or is doing – to the Messiah, her King. Now I don't see, if all these things *have to happen*, as he says, how the people who are to do them have any real choice. If God and Christ can foretell what's going to happen in a nation in the future, they can just as easily foretell what's going to happen in a man's mind and soul, which doesn't seem to leave a lot of room for this personal freedom and moral choosing you're jawing about. Whether Ezekiel said so or not!"

James holds Philip's gaze, pausing before he speaks. "Look, Philip, the point is, if you'll stop worrying and pray, you're safe. That's all."

Peter nods vigorously. "See, we do agree on some things, brother. He's right, Philip – and anyone else who is afraid. Have faith, and no harm can come to you. Jesus our Lord and Master says so. It must be so, for he would not lie to us."

Philip leaps up. "I'm not afraid, I'm facing facts! And why not, damn it! He has already said we'll *all* lose our faith tonight."

He storms about in the center of the clearing again. "But never mind that – why *can't* you be harmed even if you have faith? Are you saying all the Jews who ever died at the hands of savage heathen were faithless and wicked? No, Jesus would not lie, no indeed. Now he has already said that one of us is his betrayer. Suppose he said, James, that *you* – no, you've turned to God, you're safe – here: ah, that's nice: that it is your destiny to *kill* his betrayer, who happens to be your brother, John. No – just consider it!"

James is shaking his head with a twisted grin. Philip regards him for a moment; then his eyes dart from side to side as he speaks again. "But wait, that's too simple. Let's imagine that a strange turn of events 'throws you into a moment' which indicates unquestionably that, if you are to choose what is good and right, you must choose to stab your beloved brother in the back – no, slit his throat – and at your mother's table! What would you do?"

James scoffs and looks aside. Philip grins.

"Don't think it's impossible, James. In this moment one of us, Jesus's closest and dearest, is destined to choose to betray him. It is possible, James. And it would be like going to hell for you, wouldn't it? What would you do? Say, 'Sorry, I do not want to do that. You'd better find someone else'? *Sure* you would.

"'Do what you have to do.' That is it. Right there. What do we do? Not what we want, not what we choose, but what we have to do. Sure, I admit it – I was losing control a few moments ago. But who of us has control? Who of us is in control?"

Philip whirls to face Peter but doesn't approach him.

"And you, Simon Peter! You talk about having faith! He's already insisted twice tonight, despite your protests, that you will *deny him three times* before the cock crows. And I don't imagine the cocks will lose their voices any time soon. Is that what you imagine, Peter?

"You sit there like the hard old stone you are, thinking it's impossible, you couldn't deny him, how can it be? You protested: 'I'll die with you, Lord, before I disown you.'" Philip doesn't take his eyes off Peter. "James, you've known Peter all your life. Do you really think Peter, in his 'personal freedom before God's countenance,' will actually *choose* to deny his Lord and Master? Three times in succession? You know he won't. But do you doubt it will happen? Oh no. No, indeed. Peter may, because he's so stubborn, but you don't. Nor do any of the rest of us. Not after what we've seen, not for a moment."

Philip stops. No one talks. Peter is glowering, looking away. Philip eyes him again. "Listen, Peter, never mind denying him – what if he'd told you that *you* are his *betrayer*? You who talk as if you worship his every word – what if he'd said *that*? That you are condemned to hell! A devil! Better off unborn! On a whim of God's, you, Peter, Rock of the Church, can be extinguished from the universe! How do you know all this isn't a gigantic scheme directed by your Jesus himself to do just that, or worse, to consign you to the pits of hell? Maybe God is *bored* with your piety, Peter. How do you know? How do any of us *know?*"

Philip surveys the group, pursing his lips. No one returns his glance. He continues. "One thing seems inevitable: One of us is going to be destroyed, and not necessarily Judas. No one knows who, no one knows why – except to fulfill some moldy prophecies – but all the petitions to God of a thousand righteous Levites cannot save that person from his destruction any moment now.

No matter whether he's turned to God, no matter how much faith he has in Jesus, he is doomed, 'for all that must happen will happen' . . . and we know who said that . . . and it could be any one of us."

"Stop it, Philip!" Bartholomew shrieks. "That's enough. Just stop, do you hear me?"

"I wanted to make my point." Philip exhales as he resumes his seat. He puts his elbows on his knees and his head in his hands. "God, how I wish it weren't so." He lets out a long sigh. "I love him too, you know. Much as anyone else."

Peter's head is resting on his forearms, his face hidden.

James struggles to reply. "You've made your point, Philip. But you're being . . . well, inconsistent. Just a moment ago, accusing Thomas and Judas; now – I don't understand how you can be so unsure of the state of your soul, unless . . . you may be the one – yourself? Or . . . perhaps you've already laid plans – and now regret them?"

"*No*, I do not regret anything!" Philip's voice stabs the air. "*No,* I have not laid any plans! But *yes*, I very well *may be* the one to betray Jesus! I hope it is someone else. But I do have my doubts. I don't understand why he is doing what he's doing. I don't understand why he's so intent upon his own destruction. It makes me wonder about the whole thing. And I do not know what that wondering, that doubt, may lead me to do. But I do not pretend otherwise. I don't obscure those truths with holy pieties, holy quotes, or holy images of myself. I am not, to use a recent favorite, a *hypocrite!*"

James says nothing. Philip turns away, fuming.

Bartholomew is rubbing his temples. "He's right." Then he adds, "I don't mean about James, I mean that the Master has been using that word 'hypocrite' a lot lately, especially against the Pharisees. He's been saying the harshest things we've ever heard him say, lately."

"Mm," Andrew nods. His voice is thin, almost cracking. "All those condemnations and terrible prophecies about the end of time. Wailing and grinding of teeth."

Matthew agrees. "Sounds as if the end of time is going to be any day now. 'The present generation will see it all.'"

"Yes," Bartholomew says, "but he also talks about it as the end of the age. Ages last hundreds of years, or more."

"Maybe the age is just now coming to an end," Matthew replies.

"Maybe," Bartholomew persists, "but that's not what some astrologers I know are saying. Don't look at me that way, Matthew! These men are Persian astrologers of the caliber of the Magi, the ones who saw Jesus's star and followed it to Bethlehem, when he was born. And they say right now an age is just *beginning*, not ending."

"Perhaps Jesus came too late," Andrew offers, forcing a laugh. "And don't you look at me *that* way, James Alphaeus! I was only joking." He walks over to the western side of the clearing where he can huddle closer with Matthew and Bartholomew. "Whenever the end does come, anyway, it's going to be a terrible time. Portents in the sun, moon, and stars. Nations warring, insurrections, great earthquakes, famines, plagues."

Matthew shakes his head. "He said Jerusalem is going to be encircled by foreign powers and trampled."

James Alphaeus is outside their circle, still seated on the far other side of the clearing. He almost shouts across at them. "Even before that, we'll suffer terribly from God's hand. The Lord said we'll be persecuted, flogged before kings and synagogues, and put in prison."

Andrew darts a glance at James Alphaeus. "But won't that be as a test of our allegiance to him as our Master? It won't be punishment."

"We get only what we deserve," James Alphaeus intones. "'As we sowed, so we'll reap.'"

"And we'll be betrayed," Bartholomew whispers, "by our own friends, even our brothers!"

They all look at one another, then avert their eyes. Peter has been praying in earnest, evidently taking no heed of the conversation. Philip and Thomas have been listening in from time to time, Thomas often rolling his eyes and shaking his head, Philip with ears cocked and an odd smile.

During the break in conversation, James Alphaeus stands. His back rigid, his arms unmoving, he walks in front of Peter and Thaddeus to take a seat on a flat rock a few feet from Matthew.

James, now by himself on the far left, appears to be lost in thought. So do Simon and John, sitting on their respective rocks on the other side of the clearing, behind Bartholomew and Andrew. John's face is turned from the sight of the others, back and away from the gathering. He seems oblivious to their silence.

For a few more moments no one speaks. Then Matthew tries to resume his discussion with Andrew and Bartholomew. His voice is hushed. "'The abomination of desolation.' Everyone in Judaea having to take to the hills."

James Alphaeus blurts in again. "We won't even have time to go into our houses to get a coat. 'And alas for women with child in those days.' He told us to pray the end doesn't come in winter. He said those days will bring distress such as has never been until now since the beginning of the world which God created – and will never be again!"

"I'll never forget the way he looked when he said that," Andrew says. He sucks in his breath, shaking his head. "His eyes shining but almost mad, almost – demonic. And that is going to happen any time now."

"And it will be so bad," James Alphaeus nods, eyes gleaming, "that nothing could have survived it, if the Lord had not cut short the time of distress!"

Matthew frowns at James Alphaeus, then directs his words to Andrew. "But he told us all this to *forewarn* us. God's going to cut it short so we *can* survive it. And he gave us all those warnings about false prophets so that we would be *ready* for the Son of Man when he comes in the clouds."

"What?" Andrew asks.

Bartholomew nods. "Yes. He said that as soon as the distress was passed, the sun would be darkened, the moon would refuse to shine, the stars will fall from the sky, and the celestial powers will be shaken in heaven! I guess everything will become terribly, unbearably dark, blacker than the pit. Then he said they will see a sign, and then the Son of Man coming – "

"First they will make a great lamentation," James Alphaeus cuts in. "Then they will see him coming."

"Yes." Bartholomew frowns, prodding his side. "Coming in the clouds of heaven with great power and glory. He'll blow on his trumpet, send out his angels, and gather his chosen from the four winds, from the farthest bounds of heaven and earth. And he said, when all this begins, stand upright and hold your heads high, because your liberation is near."

Now James Alphaeus knits his brow. "I don't remember *that*. I remember he told us to stay watchful and awake, because when the Son of Man comes, he'll separate the men of all nations like sheep and goats. The ones on his right hand, the righteous, will enter eternal life, and the new age will begin. But the five foolish girls whose lamps burned out and the useless servants on his left will all be cursed and thrown into eternal fire!"

Still perched on the rock above them, Thomas stifles a laugh.

"He said all that then?" Bartholomew asks.

"Yes! *I know,*" James Alphaeus says. "He was looking right at me."

Matthew says, reluctantly, "It's true. He did."

"That's odd," Bartholomew muses, "because I don't remember it at all." He faces Matthew. "But *I know* he spoke of our liberation, because he said that looking right at *me.*"

As Matthew, Andrew, and Bartholomew exchange frowning glances, Simon, still scowling into the distance, rises and begins pacing about in the bushes in the background. Meanwhile, Thomas jumps down, walks over to Matthew, and stops, waiting for the three of them to give him their attention. "Perhaps," he says slowly, "He didn't really say any of it. Perhaps you're all just imagining the whole scene."

Bartholomew looks away. "Thomas, this is no time to play the fool."

"Don't insult me," Thomas snaps. "I'm serious. What if I were to tell you I don't remember any of this – this raving. When did he say it, anyway?"

"A couple of nights ago," Bartholomew says, "on the Mount of Olives."

James Alphaeus nods assent. Simon, still brooding and paying no heed to the conversation, resumes his seat. He reaches down to pick up a dry stick and then begins rapping it against his rock, looking away.

Matthew turns to see what the noise is, then adds, "Yes, I agree with Bartholomew."

Andrew's brow is furrowed. He moves over to lean against the large boulder. "Hmm. I thought he said those things on the Mount, but only to Peter, James, John, and me. I was wondering where all of you heard them."

Sitting apart from them a few feet, Thaddeus has been listening all along. "And I thought" – his voice cracks, and he clears his throat – "I thought he had said parts of it here and there all along our last journey to Jerusalem."

Thomas raises an eyebrow. "Then it wouldn't be 'foolish' for me to suggest that he never said a word of it to anyone!"

Matthew says, "Thomas . . . please. This is strange. Maybe the others remember."

Peter is still absorbed in prayer. John has just begun to pray a moment ago, and James's eyes are also closed, in either deep reflection or supplication. Simon continues knocking with his stick. Philip is still off to the side, either fuming or gloating as he unobtrusively listens in.

"Philip!" Matthew catches his eye. "You heard us – when did Jesus say all that?"

"Just two nights ago," Philip says, adding, with a smile, "and to all of us, of course."

Matthew eyes him for an instant, then looks toward

the others. "Simon! Do you remember?"

"Remember what?" Simon is sullen. "Oh . . . all that." His voice goes flat. "He's been talking about that for several days now, hasn't he? On the road to Jerusalem, some at the Mount of Olives?"

No one replies. Thomas and Philip grin at each other. Simon shrugs and returns to his stick and his distant gaze.

"That," Andrew says, "is strange." He holds one hand to his belly again, the other to his mouth.

"Oh, I don't know," Bartholomew shrugs. "We've all been sorely beset lately, and it's not the first time we've disagreed about things like this."

James looks up at them. "Hm? What's strange?"

''We can't agree," Andrew says, "about when and where and to whom the Master delivered his revelations about the end of time."

James is quick. "I know he told me and John and Peter and Andrew some things at the Mount of Olives the other night. Right, Andrew? I remember that vividly."

"Right, James," Philip says.

"So strange!" Andrew shakes his head.

"Yes," James nods, "and terrible too. But never mind the end of time – I can't even fathom what's going to happen right now."

Matthew gesticulates. "Why, the end is as likely to come right now as it is in a million years! He said no one knows when it will happen – not even he, the

Son; only the Father!"

"Yes," James agrees, "but certain things have to happen to the Son before then. All that about being handed over to the foreign power, flogged, mocked, and killed, and then rising from death. Not to mention various things the Prophets said must happen, which have not. At least, not in ways that I can see."

All are quiet. In the silence Bartholomew looks to James and others, a question in his eyes.

"Could we recall some of those prophecies again now? Not the commonly known ones – the land has been buzzing like the talk of bees with them for years – but I mean the more obscure ones?"

Matthew laughs. "*I* don't know any of them, Bartholomew, except the ones Jesus turns around and says he's just fulfilled!"

Thomas nods in earnest. "Also, Bartholomew, you and Andrew and James Alphaeus – and you, too, James – you didn't start poring over the books until after Jesus came to us. The only people who *knew* the prophecies were the scribes and lawyers, and they didn't pay any attention to them. The rest of us weren't waiting for the Messiah with thoughts of Scripture. We were waiting with dreams of no more work, no more oppression, and too much food!"

"True enough, Thomas," James muses. "But I can recall a few of them. My mind isn't working well now, but nevertheless: Now, Isaiah refers to a young virgin woman bearing a son, whom she will call Immanuel, who will be a light in the darkness and a Prince of Peace who will rule on David's throne. This would take place in terrible times, the people in great dread and panic. And one would arise in the House of David with the Lord's spirit of wisdom and compassion upon him, who 'shall not judge by what he sees nor decide by what he hears' – I don't understand that – but shall judge the poor with justice and slay the wicked with a word. (I haven't seen the Master kill anyone yet.) And it says that in those times the fiercest of animals shall lay down with the meekest and live in peace, and a little child shall lead them – "

"I certainly haven't seen that yet!" Matthew says.

"None of us have," Bartholomew agrees. "Isaiah also talks of only a small remnant of Israel who would turn to the Lord and Messiah at that time. That must be us and the others, though" – his voice loses its authoritative tone – "of course, the Essenes say *they're* the remnant and actually there will be *two* Messiahs."

"Come, Bartholomew," Andrew scoffs, "we're confused enough already. Why don't you go ahead, James."

"Yes," James says, then pauses. "Well . . . there's more in Isaiah, and in Jeremiah, but I'm not really sure of it. Now in Ezekiel and other places also, there are many references to the Messiah as a purifying, life-giving stream of water."

"Don't talk about water," Thomas says, grimacing. "I'm thirsty enough as it is, and I have a terrible taste in my mouth." He flops to the ground at the base of the boulder.

James is too intent to notice Thomas's gibe. "I'll be done in a minute. Ezekiel prophesies that this new stream, from which all creatures shall draw new life – and Jesus always speaks of being the source of new life, of eternal life – remember what he told the Samaritan woman at the well? Anyway, Ezekiel's prophecy seems to indicate that the Messiah will also make the Dead Sea become sweet and pure!"

Simon has been listening with growing interest. He says, "And that certainly hasn't happened yet."

"No, at least not that we know of," says James. "Now Daniel refers to a 'Son of Man' coming on the clouds of Heaven and receiving everlasting power from the Most High. And Jesus does refer to himself as the Son of Man. Micah says Bethlehem will be the birthplace of a 'Governor of Israel' who shall be their shepherd in God's Name and whose greatness shall reach the ends of the earth. Now while it is true that Jesus was born in Bethlehem and refers to himself as the 'Shepherd' – "

Simon can't hold back. "He hasn't yet become a governor for Israel, and it doesn't look like he's planning to, right?"

"Yes; that's it," James says. "Micah also refers to him as a man of peace" –

"But Jesus says he has come to bring the sword," Simon shouts, "not peace!"

"True," says James. "Well, let me finish.

"Micah ends his writing by beseeching the Shepherd to show miracles. He refers to his forgiving the sins of the faithful 'remnant' and not raging in anger forever, but delighting in eternal love. But he finishes by saying, 'You will show good faith to Jacob, unchanging love to Abraham, as You did swear to our fathers in days gone by.' Now 'Jacob' means the House of Israel, the children of Abraham, so it seems to me he could be speaking only to God the Father here, for it was God Himself who swore the Covenant. So I don't understand that, either."

Bartholomew speaks. "But Jesus did say, 'Before Abraham was, I am.' You seem to be presenting a case against Jesus being the Messiah, James. What about the prophecy of Zechariah that he fulfilled the other day, that the King of Israel would enter Jerusalem on the foal of an ass?"

"Good example," James says. "It also says the Messiah, humble and a man of peace, would banish chariots and war-horses and bows from the Land, from existence even; and he would rule the world peaceably. *That* has not happened."

"How do you know he won't still do all that?" Bartholomew asks.

"He may," James allows, pausing, "but that will be the greatest miracle yet. He's also told us the hour of his deliverance to the foreign power is imminent, and that he will be killed and rise from death on the third day to ascend to the Father."

Andrew shudders. "Do you think he'll *really* give himself up to be killed by the Romans?"

"And that he'll be mocked, and spat upon, and crucified?" Thaddeus asks.

James is in his element. "Well, Zechariah also talks of his being pierced and of all Jerusalem mourning him; and Isaiah – who also talks of the herald, who we take to be Elijah reborn as John the Baptist – Isaiah speaks of the Messiah as a servant despised and tormented for us, as a lamb led to slaughter, stricken to death, sacrificed, with our guilt laid upon him by the Lord though he had done no violence and spoken no treachery; and then this same servant bathed in light and vindicated forever." James belches.

"Do you think that means . . . " – Bartholomew is puzzling – "that Jesus somehow becomes the lamb that we . . . sacrifice and eat at Passover?"

James shrugs and sighs. "I know this: The lamb that we ate tonight may be sacrificed, but it's not dead. It's still kicking around in my bowels like – like Jonah in the whale . . . except angrier."

"No, wait," Bartholomew says, "He said that the *bread* was his flesh, not the lamb. And the wine was his blood. But I'm confused. Do you remember, a couple of times the Pharisees came asking for a sign, and he gave them the sign of Jonah? Saying he would go into the bowels of the earth for three days, even as Jonah went into the whale, and would similarly return to life?"

James doesn't reply. Andrew glares at Bartholomew again, then addresses James. "Just tell us about the prophecies, James, and let's leave it at that."

"All right," James says. He stretches and tries to find some comfort on his boulder. "And hear me, I'm not trying to prove anything one way or another.

"I remember now that the next verse of Zechariah, like Isaiah's, speaks of a barren woman husbanded by the Lord of Hosts and delivered of a Holy Child, Israel's Ransomer. That woman may well be Mary, mother of Jesus: So there's a prophecy fulfilled, if the legend is true. It's just that there *are* prophecies that haven't been fulfilled, so I want to wait and see."

"I still find fault, James," bristles James Alphaeus. "You picture the Messiah too much as a Prince of Peace, or much less, as a man despised and humbled. Haven't you read the Psalms of Solomon which say that, almighty in power, he will 'break the pride of sinners like so many pots'?" Rising to his feet, James Alphaeus punches the air with his fist as he speaks. "Ezra compares him to a devouring lion; Baruch compares his coming to earthquakes, fire, and famine for all save the elect. Our Lord is no mild lamb to be pitied, he is a mighty and terrible Lion! You watch, he will wreak his vengeance upon the wicked!"

Simon also is brandishing a fist. "Yes! Yes!"

James, however, is not moved. "The Scriptures say that too, James Alphaeus; I didn't mean to only present one side. But where have you got that nonsense? It's been determined that those men did *not* speak the Word of God, and that their books are not holy Scriptures."

"How do you know, James?" Bartholomew also is on his feet. "Because the rabbis told you so? But you, James Alphaeus, you have to admit that Jesus is constantly preaching humility, meekness, and love. What about the Sermon on the Mount? You can't keep hiding in that shroud of terror and fire, because that's just not the heart of what Jesus says."

He sits, as Thomas leaps up. "Yes!" he cries. "Right! So now let's speak of what Jesus himself says and what *he* means by it all. You've said, James, that the prophets were armed with visions of the future only to pierce the people's hearts with fear of God, right now. So they would do what he requires, right now. If the Master is going to die soon, I want to know what I'm supposed to do *now* to be saved; but I swear by God my mind is gone blank from all this burro's braying about prophecies!"

On the far western side of the clearing, Philip shouts, "Yes! Exactly!" He kicks up some dust. "I nearly fell asleep, with all that cloud and vague mist floating about. Only I'm afraid, Thomas, that there is one person here who doesn't need to worry about being saved" –

"Philip!" Thaddeus shrieks. *"Must* you – "

"Well," Philip says, "it's not like we're supposed to forget about that, hm?"

As Philip and Thomas take seats in the partial

shadows cast by tree limbs, Peter stands from his boulder in the center of the clearing. His limbs are still stiff from the fixed attitude of his praying. He glances at Philip. "No, but there's no point scraping it like Dead Sea salt over open wounds, either, Philip. I too agree with Thomas. If we cannot all pray – Lord, please forgive us – then let us speak of what he has commanded us. I would mention to several of you that he has commanded us not to swear about anything or by anything or anyone, and especially not by God, Thomas!"

Thomas turns away. "Well, I slipped, that's all."

"But, brother," Peter says, "He knows that none of us, after witnessing and partaking in even the least part of his glory, will really be willing to *seek* evil again. What he cautions us about is just what you say, slipping into it without real intention."

James Alphaeus is still standing. "That's right! Remember what he said two nights ago on the Mount: Be watchful and awake, for you don't know when the Bridegroom is coming to separate the sheep from the goats!"

Bartholomew can take no more. "You know, James Alphaeus, you *really*" –

"*Brothers!*" Andrew interjects. "Look, let's speak of something we all remember, without dispute . . . I know!" He claps his hands. "Let us speak of the beginning of the Master's mission, and the Sermon on the Mount!"

Philip chuckles, but several of the others nod in agreement.

Bartholomew stands and strokes the branch of a fig tree near the central area. "I think I can remember the first part," he says. "We were talking of it recently, weren't we, Andrew? 'Blessed are the poor in spirit, for theirs is the Kingdom of Heaven. Blessed are the meek, for they shall inherit the earth. Blessed are those who mourn, for they shall be comforted. Blessed are the merciful, for they shall obtain mercy. Blessed are the peacemakers, for they shall be called the children of God.' Mmm – what were the rest?"

"'Blessed are the pure in heart,'" Andrew says, smiling, "'for they shall see God. Blessed are those who hunger and thirst for righteousness, for they shall be satisfied.' And – "

James Alphaeus chimes in, "'Blessed are those who have suffered persecution for the right cause; theirs is the Kingdom of Heaven.'"

"Yes," Andrew says. "He said many other beautiful things on the Mount, too. Like, 'Love your enemies and pray for your persecutors.' And if someone slaps your right cheek, offer him your left."

Thomas looks on in disbelief. "Ah, here we go. Andrew, does he *mean* we're actually not supposed to defend ourselves from attack? And – what are we supposed to go around in mourning for? What does it mean to be 'poor in spirit'? *How* are the meek going to inherit the earth?"

Andrew looks at Thomas and sighs. "Thomas, we've argued his meanings round and round for three solid years. For now, why don't we just try to recall his main teachings and let each arrive at his own interpretation?"

Peter opens his mouth as though to speak – but doesn't.

"Fine," says Thomas, "I'll be glad to recall a whole storehouse full of his teachings for all of you and remind you that they drive you to hellish confusion."

"Uh oh," Matthew mutters. "Here we go, is right."

James nods. "Me too. Like, from the Sermon, the one about the body's lamp being the eye, and if the eye be *single*, the body will be full of light." He raises his eyebrows and shakes his head.

Bartholomew, meanwhile, shakes his own head. "But isn't it obvious that he is speaking of the spiritual eye of wisdom and light, which the prophets call the 'morning star' or 'star of the East'? The wise men of the East talk of it, too. Haven't we all felt that eye open, especially in prayer with him?"

Peter, though praying, looks up to speak. "We've all felt and seen much, by his grace, Bartholomew. But more likely he means something simple and practical: that you should only look to him for light."

"Then what does he mean," James Alphaeus asks, "by saying that if your hand or eye offends you, you should cut it out, for it's better to live blind than die by sight?"

Thomas laughs. "Maybe *that's* how to get a single eye. But how are we supposed to gain our lives by losing them? If he's going to raise us like he did Lazarus, why die at all?"

"Must be some deeper meaning," James says. "And we don't know it, but nevertheless to receive one of us is to receive Jesus himself, and to receive him is to receive the Father. I never understood that, but I said it in every house I entered while we were walking about and spreading his Gospel." He shakes his head once more. "I said a lot of things I'd heard but didn't understand; some, I didn't even know if I really – believed. I imagine we all said a lot of things like that."

Thomas jumps up and hangs for a moment from a tree limb, then falls to the ground again. "James, if you have ears to hear, then hear. Remember, you can tell a tree by its fruit. And the fruit never falls far from the tree!"

"Jesus never said that." Bartholomew frowns.

"I know," Thomas says, "but it sounded good."

Several of the others laugh, but James Alphaeus bristles. "Out of your own mouth you will be acquitted, Thomas, and out of your own mouth you will be condemned."

"Help!" Thomas yelps. "Well said, Alphaeus! You're right, I've never spoken a true word – including these!"

The others' laughter draws a scowl from Peter.

"This is no time for frivolity, brothers," he says. "Thomas, you spoke a moment ago – and I think you meant it – about your need for salvation. Why don't we all seriously try to recall the teachings our Lord has given about salvation, about entering the Kingdom of Heaven?"

For several moments no one talks. Finally Thaddeus ventures to speak.

"Once, out near the sea, he said the Kingdom is like a mustard-seed – the smallest of seeds, but when grown up, bigger than any tree."

Thomas, prowling about and smirking, swings onto a branch of a tree just back of the clearing. "Yes, vultures and foxes come and roost in it, the old mustard tree. But the Son of Man has nowhere to lay his head."

Peter ignores Thomas. "He also said then that the Kingdom of Heaven is like treasure lying buried in a field. The man who found it buried it again, and for sheer joy went and sold all he owned and bought the field."

Thomas shakes his head, rolling his eyes; Philip laughs. The two of them exchange glances with James as James Alphaeus says, "The Kingdom of Heaven is like a net let down into the sea, and all kinds of fish were caught in it, and it was taken to shore, and the fishermen collected the good fish and threw the worthless away. He told us that is how it will be at the end of time!"

"Hah!" Philip snorts. "Never miss a cast of the net, James Alphaeus! Now the seed of the Kingdom is sown either on a footpath, on rocky ground, among thistles, or in good soil; but it gives great increase only in good soil." He kicks up some dust. "This stuff won't even grow grass or grapes, much less a Kingdom of Heaven."

James laughs. "Well, *we* are the fishermen, so we must be the good soil."

"Ha!" Thomas jumps from the tree. "No, James, you're the weeds and you'll be burnt; but we're the wheat and we'll be eaten!" He presses his belly and groans. "No, that's not right, either, for remember: Christ alone is the bread of life, and his blood is the best wine!"

"Brothers, please!" Peter shakes both fists, at no one in particular. "This is no time for laughter!"

James looks at him with a grin. "But we're in earnest, Peter. What does he mean by that little riddle? Are we to drain him and" – he pauses to gesticulate – "chop him into little pieces after he dies? There still won't be enough for the whole world. Obviously he's talking in symbols. But how is it going to work?"

"Maybe," Bartholomew says, "in some mystical way he will divide himself like he did the loaves and the fishes, so everyone could eat."

Thomas, nearby, leans over and speaks into Bartholomew's ear with a loud whisper. "He's going to be *dead*, Bartholomew."

Bartholomew pulls away. "If he can raise other people from death, do you really think he is going to let himself die?"

James lurches to his feet, gesturing. "*He* said he is

going to! He has said so many times!" He turns to confront Peter. "Look, Simon Peter, don't be so high and mighty and outraged! Don't be so grave! Remember, if you're not like a little child, you can't enter the Kingdom. Right? *What?* He's in the Father, but the Father is in him; and he's in us, and we're in him. *Huh?* We don't know what he is *talking about* most of the time, Peter! And it does get a little ridiculous, you know. If every scrap the master throws his dogs is – is – is wrapped tightly in linens and dipped in bronze beforehand, you can't expect the dogs to keep on leaping at them with the same old solemn saliva!"

James laughs with Thomas and Philip, who adds, "And the Lord knows we've certainly had our teeth cracked a few times!"

Thomas pretends to offer Philip food, then to snatch it away. "Don't worry, the day will come when you needn't eat at all: for man cannot live on bread alone, but on every Word of God."

A bit awkwardly, James pantomimes his own words. "And then," he says, "as a starving beggar, you may come into the banquet with Abraham, Isaac, and Jacob in the Kingdom of Heaven. None of the invited guests will come, owing to previous obligations; but the servants will drag you in from the highways and hedgerows, and you will feast on the blood and flesh of Jesus!"

Philip steps forward, also play-acting. "But when

you eat the Passover Seder, remember not to dip into the bowl. As he said tonight, though, the wine is the blood of the Covenant, his blood, shed for many – so drink it down for salvation!"

"And do not fast, friends of the bridegroom," Thomas warns, "until the bridegroom is taken away from you. *Then* you had better fast!"

"But if it's on the Sabbath," Thaddeus chimes in, "you can . . . you can have an ear of corn!"

Thomas, Philip, and James laugh. "Perfect, Thaddeus!" Thomas says. "Fresh skins for new wine!"

James, loosening up, adds, "When you eat and drink, don't just clean the outside of the cup and dish; it's unclean, and hypocritical besides. Clean the inside first, and then the outside will be clean, also."

"For remember" – Philip stifles a belch – "it is not what goes inside a man's mouth that defiles him, but what comes out. For what goes in passes through the bowels and comes out below; but what comes out, comes from the heart; so if evil comes out, there is evil within you – in your heart!"

He whirls, taking Thomas's chin in one hand. "But the Kingdom itself is within you! Did you eat it? Don't let it pass out! But don't worry, for I tell you this: There are some of those standing here who will not *taste death* before they have seen the Son of Man coming in his Kingdom!"

Several of the others jump to take their stand, chortling and clapping; all laugh except James Alphaeus, Peter, and John, who has paid no attention the whole time. Peter suddenly looks up, startled.

"*Silence!*" His voice cracks like thunder; the others are instantly motionless. "Stop your laughter! Listen!"

Thomas grins. "What, Peter? Did you just see him coming in his Kingdom?"

Peter doesn't even look in his direction. "Silence your blasphemy, Thomas! *Listen!*"

All are quiet, listening. No one moves or even changes expression.

John speaks softly. "He's crying."

"Who?" Philip asks. "I don't hear it."

There is silence.

"It's . . . it's Jesus." Peter is speaking as if to himself. "He's crying. Our Lord is weeping!"

"Oh . . . Master!" Bartholomew cries. "*Weeping?*"

Peter is craning his ear toward the hill behind them, to the south. "Wailing, even! Our Lord Jesus Christ is weeping on that hilltop!"

All listen in the stillness.

"Jesus . . . " Thomas says, his mouth muffled by his cloak.

Peter and Bartholomew burst into quiet tears. James Alphaeus sobs, as does Matthew. Thomas, dry-eyed, buries his head. The others sit in silence, bowing their heads.

"Why?" James asks, in a whisper. "Why is he weeping?"

Philip's reply is quiet but harsh. "Maybe he doesn't *want* his blood shed for many."

Thomas agrees. "He really doesn't *want* to die!"

"He's probably praying," Philip goes on, "not to have to go through with it. As strong as he is . . . weeping." He sighs. "Ours is a cruel God."

James frowns. "You mean even *he* 'has to do what he has to do'?"

Peter looks up violently, his eyes wet. "Nonsense! *Blasphemy!* He's up there weeping for us, sinners that we are, not for himself! He is crying for the world!"

"Yes!" Tears are streaming down Bartholomew's face. "He is weeping for us, because we're so wicked that we lie about and laugh even as his hour approaches."

"Master," Andrew mutters, beseeching, "forgive us."

Some sob on, others sit in silence, some pray. Philip and Thomas each return to their original seats, at opposite sides of the clearing. After a couple of moments, they all compose themselves.

"Is he still . . . ?" Philip asks, softly.

"No," Peter says. "I don't believe he is."

"Thank God," Bartholomew sighs. "I don't think I could have borne it much longer."

"He's wept before," James says. "Don't you remember? As we entered Jerusalem?"

"I couldn't bear it then, either," says Bartholomew.

Peter glares at them all. "Brothers! I *beg* of you – let us not start bickering or laughing or blaspheming again. He told us to *pray*. If he's up there weeping for our miserable souls, the least we could do is pray for ourselves. We all know in our hearts the prayer he has given us. There can be no disagreement. Can we not now pray together, before the Father Himself and in Jesus our Master's name?"

Most kneel or sit at once to pray. A few others, making gestures of discomfort, soon do the same. Only Philip and John do not join in. The voices of the Apostles are thin, quavering, sometimes broken by a sob, as they invoke:

"Our Father,
Who art in Heaven,
Hallowed be Thy name.
Thy Kingdom come,
Thy will be done,
On Earth, as it is in Heaven.
Give us this day our daily bread,
And forgive us our trespasses,
As we forgive those who trespass against us.
And lead us not into temptation,
But deliver us from evil,
For Thine is the Kingdom,
And the Power, and the Glory,
Forever and ever. Amen."

Some continue praying, others sit quiet, their faces as if hooded. A breeze plays in the leafless branches of several of the trees, prompting Andrew and some of the others to draw their cloaks tighter around themselves. Matthew alternately pulls at his beard and runs his fingers through his hair and across his scalp. Bartholomew sits in the dust, staring, his face ashen in the pale light. No one stands or moves very much for a long time.

Hunched over in the dust, Thaddeus glances at each one of the others, eyes darting. Finally he clenches his fists and sits upright, with an outburst:

"I can't stand this any more! You're right, Peter! I can't stand any more discussing or bickering or baiting. But I can't stand this waiting, either! I can't stand the fear and the prayers! I can't stand this wretched freezing garden, and I can't stand the dark!" He leaps to his feet and takes three steps toward the path leading out of the garden at the left rear of the clearing, then turns to face the others, his chin trembling as he shouts at them. "I can't endure this any more, do you hear? I won't! I'm going to leave, I tell you!"

Peter says, "Thaddeus, brother, sit down. You can't leave."

"Who said I have to stay?" Thaddeus shouts. "Why *can't* I leave?"

"The Lord Jesus himself said so," Peter replies. His voice is soothing but firm. "Don't you remember, at the gate? 'Stay here and pray until the hour has come.'"

Thaddeus shouts again, "So what? Listen" – his eyes are flashing, his lips and chin still trembling – "I renounce him as the Lord! I renounce him as my Master!

I decided to join him. Why can't I decide to leave this madness?"

Everyone looks at him. No one breathes.

"If you leave, Thaddeus," Philip says, his voice as soft as Peter's, "where will you go?"

"I'll – I'll go back to my home town!" Thaddeus appears surprised by his own words. "I'll go back to my family! To my trade!"

Peter stands to his full height. Now his tone is darker. "*Thaddeus . . .* "

With a questioning glance, Philip looks toward some of the others, nodding his head in Peter's direction. Simon and James nod in affirmation. Simon has been sitting all the way over on the western edge of the clearing. He now rises without a sound and traces a path around the big rock until he's standing a few feet behind Peter. Though he doesn't take his eyes off Thaddeus, Peter shifts one leg and turns ever so slightly, without concern or fear, to accommodate the potential threat of Simon's presence.

"Well, Thaddeus," Philip says, still soothing, "I hope and pray you do it. If you want to leave . . . leave!"

Thaddeus eyes him for a moment. Then, hesitating, he looks around at all the others except Peter.

"All right . . . I will!" he says, his jaws clenched. He starts walking out. "I will leave!"

Peter takes two steps as Thaddeus nears the trees in the left rear of the clearing. "*Thaddeus!*" he thunders.

Thaddeus slows, then stops, just within sight on the dirt path. Philip moves closer so that he flanks Simon on Peter's other side. The two of them crouch like wrestlers, ready to restrain Peter.

"Go ahead, Thaddeus," Philip says. "We won't let him stop you." His voice hardens. "Go ahead, damn it!"

Thaddeus takes another step, and one more, then begins wringing his hands. He's still within sight. Simon moves between Thaddeus and Peter; he and Peter glower at each other.

"Don't worry about Peter, Thaddeus!" Simon says. "We'll hold him."

"I'm not," Thaddeus says, "I – I'm not worrying about . . . I – "

"Then go!" Philip growls. "Do it! *Leave!*"

"I – I *can't!*" Thaddeus cries. "I can't make myself do it! I can't even walk out a gate!" He begins to cry, slumping to the ground. "Can't even leave . . . own two feet . . . God help me, I *can't.*" He weeps, his sobs muffled in his cloak.

Peter sits down. So does Philip, on a rock near James. Simon strolls back to his rock on the other side of the clearing. Andrew goes to console Thaddeus, and, after awhile, helps him back to where he was sitting, on the ground not far from Peter.

"That's what I thought would happen," Philip says. Then he looks toward Thaddeus and Andrew. "You see, Thaddeus, you decided to join him about the way a mouse drowning in a flood decides that it's actually just paddling out for a swim. And you have about as much chance of leaving this garden now, decision or not, as that mouse has of getting out of the flood alive."

"Philip!" Bartholomew cries. "Why are you tormenting Thaddeus? Why are you so full of venom tonight?"

"Yes, Philip!" Thomas says. "Why don't *you* leave?"

Philip smiles. "Because I know *I* can't. Thaddeus thought he could; I wanted him to try. I wish he'd done it." He purses his lips and reflects for a moment. "I don't suppose there's anyone else who thinks he can leave now? No? No . . . I guess not."

"Of course not," Peter says, gravely. "And you are wrong, Philip. We're not like mice in a flood. We're more like fish in the sea." He pauses, sitting up to address the whole band.

"Once we have swum into the net of the promise of his Kingdom, we can't leave. We can't go back. We're different. We're like netted fish, we have no choice. We may still be deep under water, but in reality, we're in the net. All we can hope for now is that the Fisherman, our Lord, will boat us, cook us, and eat us quickly. And thus we will become part of him, and true fishers of men, as he promised. It's taken me three years to see what he meant by that. It is a glorious promise, but, as we see now, a terrible one. The only way we can ease the pain of it is to do as he commands. So now, brothers, please, let us pray."

Peter kneels by the big rock. Some of the others do the same, or close their eyes. No one makes a sound.

James whispers to Philip. "Well . . . here we are."

"Oh, shut up, James," Thomas says, out loud.

Andrew sighs. "I wish Judas would come back – or Jesus would come down. I wish something would happen."

There is a long silence. Several enter postures of prayer. Others try to make themselves more comfortable on the rocks.

Sitting on the ground and leaning against the big rock, Thomas begins to examine his fingernails. Then he searches the ground for a few moments until he finds a stone suitable to his needs. He picks it up and begins busily filing his fingernails with it. The sound is quite audible, and Peter comes out of silent, closed-eyed prayer to cast a dark glance at him.

In mid-stroke on a thumbnail, Thomas suddenly stops what he's doing. Without shifting his hands or his position, he smiles and turns his head to look at Peter. For a moment the two confront each other, motionless. Then, without looking away from Peter, Thomas laughs and hurls the stone over his shoulder, into the trees behind the big rock. Peter closes his eyes again.

The light is dimmer now. Matthew comes out of prayer. He looks around until he locates Bartholomew, then waits for another moment before speaking. His voice is high and tremulous, like a child's.

"Bartholomew?"

Bartholomew is just rousing himself. "Yes?"

Matthew is eager, but hesitant. "A few moments ago you were . . . reciting part of the Master's Sermon on the Mount. . . . You know, I wasn't there then – I know you've done it before, but – could you describe . . . ? What it was like? What he was like?"

Bartholomew has a dreamy look on his face. "Yes. Yes, I will. Let me think back for a moment . . . mm."

Most of the others are also listening now. As Bartholomew speaks, his face softens, and delight illuminates his features.

"You know, none of us had been with him very long then. We were all of us following him around as if we were under a spell. I remember that he just shone in those days, he glowed, there was a radiance about him such as no one had ever seen. He had walked all over Galilee, proclaiming the news of the Kingdom, curing the sick, freeing the possessed, dispensing his grace to one and all without question, often without even being asked. There were great mobs of people following him everywhere he went, not only Galileans, but Judaeans, people from Jerusalem, Decapolis, Syria, and Transjordan.

"Word of his greatness was spreading like – you've heard tales of how the river Nile floods, in Egypt? Water suddenly everywhere, just like that? That's what it was like. Suddenly everyone everywhere was whispering, 'He's come! He's come! The Messiah has come at last!' It's almost as if there wasn't time for people to carry the word from village to village, for the news seemed to travel by itself."

"That's really true," Andrew interrupts. "I remember going into villages and before I could open my mouth, people would say, 'You've come to tell us of the Christ, haven't you?'"

Bartholomew stands and begins walking slowly before them, still as though in a dream.

"Yes. Well, finally there were so many people that one day we went to him and said, 'Lord, there are so many now, they cannot all hear your words and see you.' And he smiled and said, 'Then let us go where all may hear and see at once.'"

Bartholomew points to the large boulder. "So we climbed one of the Horns of Hattin, and he sat on a boulder near the top." He gestures down the rock and across the clearing. "And there were people sitting and leaning and standing not only all over and down that hillside, but in the valleys and up neighboring hills as well. And the air was buzzing with whispers and excitement, for everyone was wondering what he would do next.

"Then he stood and raised his hand for silence" – Bartholomew raises his own right hand, palm facing outward – "and it was extraordinary, the effect he had. For not only did all the talking cease, but the birds ceased their songs, and the wind died down. And then there was only the gentle *sshhh* of a mild breeze, and then even that died away. The entire countryside was hushed, not only in perfect silence, but in perfect peace as well. I don't think there's been a moment like it, before or since."

Bartholomew looks down, reflecting. "Usually when he teaches, different people have different feelings about him and what he says – not just different the way the Pharisees differ from us, but also as we differ from each other. In the way some of us seem to hear different things than others do; in the way one will feel uplifted and joyous, and another as if he'd been scourged, after one and the same discourse by the Master.

"But on that day, on the Mount" – he lifts his face again, his eyes shining – "everyone felt perfectly at peace. Not a man moved a muscle. No one wanted to. I spoke to many people afterward, all said the same thing. There was an aura of peace that seemed to emanate from his raised hand and to pervade the entire land and every single mind and heart. It was a special day, a very special day. And then he lowered his hand" – Bartholomew lowers his own – "and began to speak.

"His voice was like – like water from a deep spring, flowing smooth and cool. Everyone heard him clearly. His words – well, you know about the Sermon. It was inspiring, chastising, magnificent, gentle, harsh, forgiving, loving all at once. Of course very few of those who heard it remembered all he said – or even most of it. Fewer still have acted on his words and become true disciples. But no one ever forgot being there. No one could ever forget the stillness, the grace of his gestures, the beauty of his features, the radiance of love which seemed to emanate from his body and set all the air tingling and penetrated every heart, so that now and then someone would close his or her eyes and let out a long, deep sigh. Some people tried to keep their eyes closed so they could listen closely. But I almost think he didn't really intend for us all to hear his words well – because you couldn't keep your eyes away from him, it was as if the whole world were expressed in his . . . I don't know how to say it; but you couldn't help just looking and looking at him, and just looking at him almost put you into a trance, he was so majestic and beautiful."

Bartholomew pauses for a long moment. "As I said, perhaps only a few remembered the words he spoke, but no one could ever forget being there. Some said later that when he ceased speaking and began walking down the hill, it was like a wave or a veil passing over everyone as he went by, and again there was noise and movement and people remembering their lives and their troubles, like waking from a beautiful, intensely real dream. But no one who was there could ever forget that dream. No. Never. I'm sure of that."

There is silence. Bartholomew's eyes continue to gleam as he gazes up and off into the distance.

"Thank you, Bartholomew," Matthew says. "That was beautiful."

The others murmur agreement. Bartholomew looks up suddenly, as if coming to.

"Huh? Oh . . . I" – he shrugs – "I just told you

what happened, like you asked."

James is musing. "'Wherever two or more of you gather in my name . . . "

"It's the truth," Thomas sighs. "It's almost as if the Master were here and told that story himself."

A gentle smile plays around Peter's mouth as he nods. "You're so right, Thomas. It's as if we had forgotten him all evening, though we've been talking all about and around him."

He rises and stretches, then cocks his head. "Reminded me, too, of what it was like when he first came to me, to me and Andrew, by the shore of the Sea. Remember, Andrew? We were at least a hundred yards out at the time, casting a net. And suddenly there was this – this *presence* all around us. And I looked to shore, busy with boats and nets and fish, but my eyes went right to him, as if pulled to him with a stout line – and he was looking straight at me. I didn't even stop to think, I leapt into the water and swam right to him. Remember, Andrew?"

Andrew smiles. "How could I forget? I had to pull in a net filled to overflowing and bring in the boat myself!"

The others laugh.

"'Stories from Scripture' time," Philip says.

"Come, Philip," Bartholomew pleads. "Don't be so dark at the mouth; it's been a long time – "

"No, no." Philip's tone is soft. "I mean, I want to hear them too."

Simon belches, then speaks, also in a gentle mood. "You talk of radiance, presence, stillness. I remember when I first saw him, I was secretly telling news of a meeting to some Zealots in a marketplace." He stands to re-enact the event.

"And he came by and heard me and looked me in the eye – and at first I feared he might be a Roman out of uniform, but he just kept looking at me. I glanced at my friends, but they didn't seem to notice anything special about him. So I looked back – and there he was, still looking me right in the eye, and exuding an overwhelming aura of power, majesty, of extraordinary strength – even though he is not a brawny man, physically. And one other thing, which may sound odd: He seemed to possess wisdom vast but also cunning.

"Then he turned and began to walk away. After we'd walked a few steps, he turned to me and said, 'You've been with them for five years; but now you must follow me.' And that was the truth. I didn't even bid farewell to my friends, and I have never seen them since."

Thaddeus is puzzled. "I thought you said you saw them once a few months later, but they wouldn't speak with you. I thought they tried to attack you."

Simon looks away, but not before his eyes betray a flash of anger. "Oh . . . yes. I'd forgotten that. They didn't attack me, though . . . but anyway, it doesn't make any difference."

"'Cunning'?" James frowns. "I've never seen that

in him. I'll tell you, when I first saw Jesus, I didn't feel that great an attraction to him at all. It's true. He called, and I came, almost lagging behind John. I remember hesitating on the beach and looking back at our father, still in the boat, standing mouth agape and still as a pillar of salt. Poor old Zebedee. He lost both his sons and had to hire new help, besides.

"But I soon began to see that Jesus was very wise and good. And one day, maybe a month later – and Bartholomew, I'm afraid I didn't really feel very much on the Mount – *but*, not long after meeting him, I happened to question him on some silly matter, and he didn't say a word but looked at me – and I felt this . . . – " James touches his fingers to his temple – "warmth pervade my mind, and I knew then that here was a man who *knew* me, and knew everything there was to be known."

"Whew!" Matthew lets out a low whistle. "Wonders and miracles!" He shakes his head. "Never happened to me. I had heard so much about him – his healings, his wisdom, his love for everyone – and I had dismissed it all as the dreams and wishes of a simple people under the Roman whip.

"But as he approached my table in the counting house that day, I found myself practically trembling in anticipation of something wondrous. Over he came, looking at me as if he were thinking, 'Looks a bit flabby but I'll take him anyway.' Then he nodded toward the door and said, 'Come, follow me,' and smiled, almost smirked at me. So I followed, expecting miracles despite myself – but none ever happened to me personally. Only this bond of love between us that keeps on growing; and that's more than enough of a miracle, for me."

Philip bursts into laughter. "Now, hold on, Matthew, you old leech! You left out the best part. I remember the time you *asked* for a miracle!"

"What's this, Matthew?" Thomas asks.

Matthew stares at Philip. "Aah, Philip, I'll reward you for this – betraying family secrets!

"All right. Nothing startling, Thomas. During one of our early journeys I was drinking a particularly rancid pitcher of goat's milk and thinking of the Master's first miracle, when he changed the water to wine at the wedding in Cana – which I hadn't been there to enjoy, naturally. Just at that moment the Master came over to me – I was standing apart aways – and there was that delicious fragrance about him that we've noticed from time to time, and he asked, eyes twinkling, if there was anything I wanted. That seemed a clear invitation, so I asked if he would transform the milk to wine."

Several of the others exclaim in surprise.

"Believe me," Matthew continues, "I was shaking so hard I could hardly stand up. But he matter-of-factly asked if there was anything else. I said no. So he smiled, and after making me promise to drink it all down without anyone else knowing about it – said he didn't want all of you demanding your share, and you know how

fussy he is telling people not to talk about his miracles –
well, he changed that milk to wine.

"The only problem was, it was the rottenest wine
I ever tasted – and I had to drink every drop, because I'd
promised. And after I was done and was feeling almost
as terrible as I feel now, he came over again, chuckled,
and said, 'Ah, Matthew. You should have asked for *good*
wine. Bad milk makes terrible wine, doesn't it?'"

They all laugh and clap.

"Matthew," James says, "you're pulling some
wonderful wine stories out of your cloak tonight. But –
how did Philip find out?"

Matthew's face sours; Philip laughs.

"I tended him all night," Philip grins, "while
he retched."

Matthew snaps, "And a perfect occupation for
such a wretch as you! But now you come clean with *your*
story, you viper!"

Philip eyes Matthew closely. Matthew smirks.

"Didn't you come to hear him speak," Thaddeus
asks, "and weren't you so impressed that you followed
– and then later you were appointed one of the Twelve,
with the rest of us? Isn't that all it was?"

Philip stands, smiling with one side of his mouth.
"All right, I suppose. Seeing as I may be dead or damned
by morning, I'll tell you what actually happened.

"Yes, Thaddeus, my joining him was just that
simple. Now you all know I'm inclined to a dark view of

things, and full of a thousand other faults, no doubt. But one that I always kept secret is that I used to . . . enjoy women, you see. And I used to get a terrific hankering – and suddenly a lovely opportunity for me to get away would present itself like a dove flying into my hand, like a door opening before me."

He takes two steps toward the trees and bushes through an opening between James and Andrew, then wheels and steps back again.

"It was uncanny, how that would happen – but even more uncanny what would happen next. Because I would go to one of my woman-friends – and, suddenly, just at the wrong moment, in some loft or brothel, I would want nothing more than to tell her about Jesus and the Kingdom."

"*You*, Philip?" Bartholomew is wide-eyed.

Philip smiles, nodding. "In fact – here's something you'll all marvel at. Guess who brought Mary of Magdala to him."

"You, Philip?" James asks.

Philip nods. "Hah, I feel almost like . . . eh, James, what was the name of Bathsheba's husband?"

"King David?"

"No, the first one."

"Oh. You mean Uriah, the Hittite. Who David got rid of."

"Yes," Philip grins. "Almost like Uriah – in a spiritual sense, of course. But as I – "

"What are you insinuating, Philip?" Peter's voice is clipped. "That Jesus knows Mary as you did?"

"Not at all." Philip regards Peter with a trace of a smile on his face. "I wouldn't insinuate he knows her any differently than he knows everyone else. What are *you* insinuating, Peter? Time was when Mary was more a wife to me than anything else. For all I know, or you either, she may now be a saint; she may be Jesus's spiritual equal; she may even be directing the whole mission!"

Peter, red-faced, is about to reply, but Philip cuts him off.

"All right, I'm joking – but I wouldn't be surprised at anything. I *am* surprised he hasn't appointed her and some of the other women apostles – he's so close and free with them."

"The Father would not have it so," Peter says, setting his jaw.

"Apparently not," Philip replies. "Well, anyway, as I was saying, now, you all know I've never been exactly a soldier at proclaiming the Gospel. But in those moments, Peter, you yourself couldn't have equalled me. It was not only embarrassing, it was frightening! After a few episodes, when that yearning came, I just ignored it or suffered it.

"And, of course, sooner or later, the Master would sneak me a knowing grin."

They all laugh. Philip sighs.

"But I still get that hankering. Strong as ever."

"You do?" Andrew asks.

"You *don't?*" Philip's eyes narrow at him.

"Well, not . . . not strong as ever, certainly." Andrew avoids Philip's gaze.

"*Maybe* not," Philip snorts. "But we all get it. We're men, not gods, despite our hopes and dreams. It's not something we can hide. The smell of a woman, the way she caresses the air with the simplest movements of her body, walking, tossing seeds onto a fresh-plowed field . . . you, Peter! I've seen you clench your fist and grit your teeth against the desire to stroke the hand of a woman lifting water to your parched lips. Or do you deny it?"

Peter looks away.

"So, let's not *pretend*, brothers." Philip regards each of the others. "The difference is that most of you persecute yourselves for wanting women, all because of what he says about adultery and cutting out your eyes; while I don't see anything wrong with it, in itself, but I can't do a damned thing about it."

There is silence. Peter turns back toward Philip. "Two questions, Philip," he says. "One, how did Matthew come to find out?"

"Heh!" Matthew laughs. "The old hard-heart sympathized with me in my drunken wretchedness and told me the whole tale – with considerably more graphic details – thinking I'd forget by morning."

Peter can't hide a smile, but his tone is sober. "Watch it now, let's not become profane. But, Philip, in the face of such a personal miracle for you – this is my second question – how can you continue to doubt that Jesus is the Christ?"

Philip strides slowly across the foreground of the clearing and paces about on the right. "Peter, those experiences were 'uncanny,' yes, but every one of us has accomplished far wilder miracles ourselves, just by saying Jesus's name over someone's leprosy!

"How do I continue to doubt?" He has a trace of a smile on his lips as he crosses his arms over his chest and raises one eyebrow. "I guess the same way Matthew continues to crave and sneak wine. Maybe it's a bad old habit, my doubting. Hah – when the Master cures gout, it's permanent; but when he cures doubt, it's only temporary. It's not like a devil that can be cast out by an incantation. It's in my own mind."

Peter is shaking his head. "Wait, Peter!" Philip says. "No preaching. Let's continue telling stories and laughing together. That does more to dispel doubts than any sermon."

There is another pause. James makes an effort to say something. "Talk of miracles . . . I guess we've seen the Master perform the greatest wonders that have ever taken place on Earth, except the miracles of God Himself."

Thomas clambers over the boulder and begins walking about in the far portions of the clearing and among the trees.

"That's true," Andrew says, shifting in the dirt next

to Thaddeus. "But the most miraculous thing is the love that he evokes in people, and their faith, which inspires him to perform them."

"You're right," Bartholomew nods. "It's almost beyond belief. They seem to have more faith than we do, though we've seen him transfigured into Light before our very eyes and blessed by the voice of the Father Himself, in the presence of Moses and Elijah."

Matthew agrees. "Mm. Even such a sign as that doesn't seem to be enough for us. And all the signs and miracles surrounding his birth, and the miracle upon the Sea of Galilee . . . it's a mystery in itself that we still find it difficult to love him as the Christ he is."

"It really is," Peter adds. "Even though he gave us the power ourselves to heal and cast out devils in his name, and we invoked it over and over again, we still find it difficult. Not only you, Philip; all of us."

Bartholomew is beatific. "While the blind accept him instantly, even before he gives them sight. He heals a withered arm; the man beams with love and says, 'You are my Lord.' Or the Roman centurion who came and said, 'Lord, if you but say the word my dying son will be cured,' and Jesus said he had never seen such faith in Israel and then cured the child, though it was twenty miles away in Capernaum."

Andrew frowns. "Wasn't he *in* Capernaum then?"

"Who knows?" Thomas asks from behind the great rock. He pauses. "Also – not to make little of the blind and the faithful, but . . . if they're so pure, why aren't they in our places?"

No one replies.

"Another remarkable thing," Andrew says, ignoring Thomas's question, "is the way he sometimes *plays*. When he first began healing, it caused me some wonder to see him sometimes start back – like this – as if in surprise at his own cure. But then he would smile at me, and I began to see he was playing. The same way he plays at being tired after many cures, as if the Son of God could really get tired!"

"Remember the time he was teaching in the countryside near Bethsaida," Matthew asks, "and we didn't have enough food? And he gave thanks, and broke a loaf of bread, and instantly it became two loaves! Remember how amused he looked?" Matthew imitates an expression of startled amazement.

Thomas is pressing his belly. When he speaks, his words sound forced. "Maybe he wasn't faking, you know? He really looked startled to me."

"Yes, and here's why," Bartholomew says. "All those people were so stunned, he *had* to pretend surprise, or they wouldn't have been able to eat! They probably would've gotten indigestion!"

Thomas belches loudly. Bartholomew either doesn't notice or chooses not to respond. "But the way he handled it, after a few moments they were all giggling when half a fish would become whole in his hand, and" – he mimics – "he'd raise his eyebrows and almost rise back off his seat. How they laughed – thousands of them, with this lovely, easy laughter rippling through them, all the while feeling how sacred the miracle was. And how he played for them! Look: break a fish lengthwise, or break off a tail, and blink! zoop! two whole fishes. More of them came to love and accept him through that meal than through all the preaching he'd done that afternoon."

"No doubt," Thomas allows. "But how can you be certain he was really feigning surprise? And why *can't* he *really* get tired, and angry, and upset, and weak, and sad?"

Thomas doesn't wait for anyone to respond.

"Listen – do you remember the woman by the lakeside who had piles? When he'd cured her, she ran around shouting, 'The Messiah is here, he's cured my piles!' Funny, yes, but do any of you remember exactly what happened when he cured her?"

Several shake their heads. Thomas moves back around the boulder and into the center of the clearing to re-enact the incident.

"I was looking at him the whole time. She came up from behind and touched his cloak, and he turned and asked of the crowd, 'Who touched my clothes?' – "

James breaks in. "Brother, you *know* he was just playing with them! You can't deny all the times he's asked questions that he subtly indicated he perfectly well knew the answers to. The times he's known our thoughts, our minds; even the Pharisees' minds."

"I don't deny that," Thomas replies. "He may even have known perfectly well who had touched him when he asked that question, I'll even grant that, but – *but* – I was looking him right in the face when that woman touched his robe. And at that instant his expression became one of utter, spontaneous surprise! She couldn't have surprised him more if she had reached up his robe and pinched him!"

"Thomas!" Peter shouts.

"Well, it's true!" Thomas shoots back. "If he faked that look, he must be the Son of God, because he was so surprised, *I* felt surprised! Even though I'd seen it all. And the woman seemed to realize she'd been cured just at that same instant, and she had that very same look of shocked surprise on her face" – he imitates her, then quickly hoists himself up to and sits atop the rock – " . . . really amazed me, the whole scene."

"I don't know, Thomas," Peter says. "I remember thinking he was really playing that time. I whispered to him, 'Master, they're crowding all around you, how can you even ask that?' And he looked at me like this – and he winked!"

The others exclaim, nod, and laugh.

"Thomas," Andrew says, "are you sure you didn't imagine that look of surprise?"

"Damn it!" Philip fumes. "Why are you always doubting Thomas's word? He was sincere enough – "

"You're one to talk, Philip," Bartholomew chides, "after your recent accusations. You choose not to doubt him now only because if he were faithful to facts it would challenge your own doubts of the Master's divinity!" He looks up. "But listen, Thomas, we don't mean to distrust you, it's just that – "

Tears are streaming down Thomas's cheeks, but his eyes flash. "Don't pride yourself on having reduced me to tears . . . I'll tell you why I'm weeping. That look of surprise on his face . . . was the first thing that awoke love for him in me – real love – and not because he's God but because he's *man!* Because it showed me that, despite all his miraculous powers, despite his all-knowingness, he is still capable of being surprised! At that moment, I felt he was the great brother of my heart. I *knew* it. . . .

"A moment after that, you saw tears running down my face, you thought it was from laughter at that silly woman and her piles? Not a bit of it, my so-called *brothers*. I have wept damned few tears out of love, and the ones I have you cannot take away from me! So you can doubt me from here to heaven, or to hell for that matter – all the rest is a *shadow* compared to the reality of that look."

He sighs. No one else has anything to say.

"For God knows if it isn't, I'd gladly say different. Because it's only on account of that look that I've borne his warnings and your taunts ever since. That I haven't just *left* this idiocy – and I could've, too! Because once I'd come to love him for being human, I could not help doubting he was divine. I just don't have the capacity to see him as the 'Son of God' and still see him the way I know him in my heart: a man, a son of man.

"It doesn't occur to you all" – Thomas pauses, glancing at several of them – "but it occurs to me that perhaps he went apart from us to pray tonight because he doesn't want to have to hold back his farts and smell ours. Now that may be vulgar, but it's *human;* it's man. He walks, talks, looks – we sometimes have had to point him out to crowds, who mistake Peter or Philip for him instead – he hungers, eats, *desires*, sweats, farts, and hums a song just like the rest of us; and he calls himself Son of Man. *You* call him Son of God. It's just not in me. I wish it were, but it's not, and that is where all the trouble comes from."

Silence. Simon picks up a stick and begins his tapping again.

"Thomas . . . oh, Thomas." Andrew exhales, then gets up and walks over to his rock next to Matthew. "You remind me of a dream I had not long ago, a dream I've almost tried to forget. I saw Jesus as a small, puny man surrounded by dark, faceless figures which were slowly moving in upon him. He was sitting there quietly but looking about through the surrounding figures like this" – Andrew assumes an expression of fear and worry – "as if he were searching for someone to help him. But no one came to his aid. Not – not even me."

Matthew places a hand on Andrew's knee. "I wouldn't worry about dreams, Andrew."

"But if he is the Lord and knows our minds," Andrew asks, "doesn't he know when we dream about him? Doesn't he give us those dreams?"

"Whew," James whistles, "make sense of all *that*, hm?"

Thomas slips down from the boulder and begins walking toward the trees in the left rear of the clearing, wiping his face on his sleeve. He looks down at James. "Still figuring it all out, James? Here's another scrap for you, then. The reason Judas and I stopped talking was that Judas began to see Jesus as 'the Lord.' And though I had confided my whole story to him and no one else, he would not tell me why."

"Madness," Philip muses. "And I never understood what he means by 'Son of Man,' either. Yes, Peter, I know; you've told me it's because he came to Earth and took birth as a human being. But if that is all he means, then he should call himself 'Son of Woman,' since they tell us he was fathered by the Lord of Hosts Himself."

Thaddeus ventures a solution. "Maybe he's both: Son of Man, Son of God. God and man."

James scoffs. "Thaddeus, don't be so simple. There must be more to it, though I'm not at all sure what it would be. He's always so full of paradoxes and parables. Like the other day, asking, 'How can the Son of David be David's Lord, in the Psalm?'"

"But don't you see?" Andrew enthuses. "All that makes no difference. Judas and I and Peter and others love him as Son of God; Thomas loves him as Son of Man; Philip just *loves* him – but we *all* love him. What did he say tonight after the Seder? 'Dwell in me, dwell in my love.' We *all*" – he flings his arms toward them in a grand arc – "dwell in his love. What else matters?"

"You're right," Bartholomew says. "Dwelling in his love . . . that's all that counts."

Andrew reflects for a moment. "It's amazing how often you have to learn that lesson. I have a confession to make – no, don't stop me, Peter! It's just that often I've been angry at one or another of you, or jealous – "

Matthew breaks in. "That's happened to all of us, Andrew. Remember the scene with James and John and their mother the other day?"

"Yes," Andrew continues, "but what I mean to say is, sometimes I'd stay angry or hurt for maybe even several days, and always, sooner or later, he'd turn and gently laugh at me, as if to say, 'Now, Andrew' – and that would pull me right out of my spite and into his love. And that's where I'd stay for awhile."

"That's happened to me, too," Thaddeus says, "when things were going all wrong or I didn't know what I was doing here. He'd just smile at me or touch me . . . his look, his touch . . . I – I guess that's why I can't leave him even if I try."

Matthew nods. "Probably. Sometimes that feeling

that he loves you and everything is all right is so sweet and thick – why, you could float on it, or dissolve in it."

Simon pauses between taps. "Or drink it, eh, Matthew?"

Matthew laughs. "Yes. Or drink it."

"At times when he" – Peter is looking at his feet as he speaks, and is struggling to get his words out – "when he has . . . chastised me, you know, often for trying too hard to please or protect him . . . well, I would feel miserable afterwards, and he would just walk by or enter the room and all the pain would disappear. It's like basking in the first strong sun after winter, or getting a beating and then being held in his embrace, like a child, and caressed until you're smiling again. Maybe crying again also, but smiling."

Simon lays aside his stick and also looks down. His speech is halting. "I'd still be . . . too embarrassed to admit it, if you hadn't said it just that way – but he actually . . . did that to me once."

The others stir and wait for Simon to go on.

"We were alone together near a well, and he asked me to draw him some water. I asked why he didn't do it himself – and he took his staff and beat me in a fury!"

In a single, swift motion, Simon grabs up a stout branch from the ground and stands, and with shocking quickness cracks it upon his rock several times.

"Beat me until I nearly passed out! You can't imagine how fierce he was." He sits, suddenly clumsy again.

"But then, afterward, he – he actually picked me up and took me onto his lap and held me."

"*You*, Simon?" Matthew is taken aback. "You *ox?*"

"Yes, me," Simon flashes a rare grin. "I asked him if I wouldn't hurt him. He said, 'Simon, I have room in my lap for millions like you."

James Alphaeus is quick to speak. "It's happened to me, too. Once I had cursed some Pharisees, and the Master turned and cursed me in the same way, but then he held me in that same way. He even kissed me."

"So wonderful," Matthew muses. "I wonder . . . what people will do – what *we* will do – when he's gone."

"Haven't there been moments," Peter asks him, "when he hasn't been physically present, but you've felt that same surge of warmth and love and joy, that presence? That's him too, you know. He'll *never* really be gone."

Matthew bites his lip, shakes his head and shrugs, and looks down and away. For a moment no one speaks.

The evening is drawing on, and the twilight is yielding to night. Several of the Apostles draw their cloaks tighter about their shoulders and huddle against the cold. After awhile Andrew stands and begins slapping and rubbing himself, and running in place for warmth. Abruptly he stops and turns to look back at John, who is still gazing off into the night. For a moment Andrew doesn't move. Then he opens his mouth as if to speak, closes it, and opens it again.

"John?" he asks, quietly.

John turns toward the group. "Yes?"

"I've never asked you," Andrew confesses, "I must admit, I've been jealous – but, what's it like to have received such an abundance of love from the Master? I've been thinking about what he said . . . he really is our Shepherd. And you're – you're his favorite. Wh – what's it like, John?"

John gives the faintest of smiles but doesn't answer. Andrew starts rubbing himself and running again.

Bartholomew holds his hands open, palms up, as he speaks. "Oh, John, open up and tell us something. You've been so silent tonight. We're sincerely curious, honestly. He's given you so much love."

John responds with little more than a whisper. "You've all . . . described the . . . feeling better than I can. He just gives it to me a lot, I guess."

Matthew's tone can't conceal annoyance. "John, don't be so – so coy. We know it's rough on you. But it's rough on all of us, and you're hoarding within you a storehouse of his grace. This is such a terrible moment, God only knows what's going to happen next. Come, John, you must share him with us."

Thomas nods in affirmation. John looks away again.

"John, you're acting like a child!" James bursts out, from the other side of the area. "Don't pretend you have no sweets in your sack. The Master's love for you isn't *yours* . . . it belongs to the whole world. Now we've never asked before – I'm your own brother and I haven't asked – but the time has come for you to share your sweets with us. Don't you think so, John?"

John whirls back toward them. "I'll tell you one thing that is clear right here, right now. These 'sweets' you're so hungry for have served at least to separate me from all of you. You're descending on me like vultures."

Andrew is sitting, huddling tight. "John! Don't say that. We're just – curious, that's all."

Thaddeus and others nod in agreement.

James addresses the others. "I know, he's still disturbed because of your fury with us over our petition the other day. That's probably why he's hardly spoken since." He turns to John. "But we've already apologized for that, John, and everyone's forgiven us."

John shakes his head, a twisted expression on his face. "My own brother speaks of me to my face as 'he.' I'm nothing but a curiosity, a special 'sweet' to the whole lot of you – "

Philip interrupts with a soothing tone. "John, John, John." He faces John but does not approach him, continuing to lean against his tree. "Listen. You're getting all flustered over nothing. All we want is for you to share with us a few of your intimate moments with the Master. That's all. Really."

John turns away. "You *don't* really want to hear about my intimate moments with him."

Peter addresses the others. "Perhaps you all

should stop pressing him – "

"No," James snaps, icily. "I don't mind admitting I am getting a little angry now. John! Why are you making such a fuss over a couple of silly anecdotes?"

John continues looking away. When he speaks, every word stings the air.

"*I said, you don't want to hear about my intimate moments with him.* You don't want to hear it."

All the others are startled. No one speaks as they stare at him. "John . . . " Andrew mutters.

Matthew sighs. "How strange!"

Even Philip backs away. "Yes, what a strange thing to say . . . "

James recovers his ire. "For the first time, I very much want to hear it! Just what are you talking about, brother?!"

John whirls around to him. *"You don't want to hear it!"*

James rushes across the clearing to John, grasps him by the shoulders, shakes him furiously, and slaps him once, hard. "Tell me! What are you talking about? *Speak*, damn it!"

With a cry, John breaks away and attempts to run off to the right. Simon and Philip catch him and wrestle him to the ground. He breaks down and weeps.

Peter looks around at the other men. "We cannot let anyone leave this place." He turns to James. "Why did you press him so hard? Couldn't you see . . . ?"

James is still breathing hard and fuming. "What's

done is done," he shoots back. He returns to his rock.

They all sit in silence. Finally, Thomas raises his eyebrows and flashes a smile.

"Here we are all over again."

"Don't you start in again!" Bartholomew shouts. "I'll go mad, I tell you."

John stops sobbing and looks up. "I will tell you what I meant."

"You don't have to," James says.

"I must," John insists. "I can't leave you to your imaginations. Just give me a moment."

He composes himself and begins speaking. His tone is deliberate but weak. He doesn't stir from the dust, and gestures only now and again, with swift, hard motions of his hands.

"There is nothing terrible, nothing scandalous, nothing dark, nothing. That's – just it. Nothing.

"I have seen others of you actually swept off your feet, knees buckling and all, by a mere smile from Jesus. But he has spent what seemed like days and weeks looking directly into my eyes with an expression of pure love and I have felt *nothing* inside. Sometimes a twinge of happiness, maybe, a flicker of affection – like the last flicker of a firefly dying in the night. Nothing more.

"'Abundance of love.' How amusing. I have received less of his love than any of you. Even the betrayer. Yes! Not since he first laid eyes on me, not since that first moment in the boat when I felt a terrific wrench in my heart and looked up and saw him standing on the sand and the light from his eyes took my breath away – yes, in that instant I lost myself in him, I was gone, there was only – this – the – eternal world of love; I – I don't know how to describe it. But – not since then. I . . . maybe I never came . . . back, I . . . . "

For a moment he is silent. The others are hardly even breathing.

"Not since then. Not on the Mount. Not – in his embrace. Not anywhere. 'Love'? He . . . he never leaves me alone. I can't feel anything. I never have. Not even when I reached him on the sand, that first day. Already I was – it was . . . too much, I" – he sighs – "I wondered who he was. I was drawn to him despite myself, like a moth to torch flames in the night. When I reached him, he said, 'Dear one, you have searched long for love; now you have found me' – and – I mean – I felt, I couldn't . . . *I . . . couldn't . . . feel . . . anything.*"

John looks at his fellow Apostles. No one will hold his glance. He shrugs, staring again at the dust by his side.

"Do you understand me? *Nothing*. There was nothing between us – even then. Or – it was all him. I –

"You all think I'm shy, or modest. I can just hear it. 'The beloved . . . like his bride.' No. Nothing. Nothing but intolerable deceit, this pretense that has nearly cracked my mind and has sucked me empty of all but the most evil feelings. And them only remaining to be drained away as well. I am draining away. I am watching myself drain away.

"What else could I do?" John's question rings loud and hovers in the silence. "I don't care if you accuse me of hypocrisy. Could I stand with him in front of a thousand suffering souls believing their Messiah is here before them at last, and, with all envious eyes upon me – including yours! – could I not return his 'loving' glance? Or could I sit in front of you all, who for better or worse have laid your souls at his feet, and tell you that his kiss upon my cheek feels like slime?

"And our 'intimate moments.' Hah! When we are not in the company of others he does not pretend. So . . . nothing happens. Except that I am expected to serve him and to show the signs of love. So . . . from our 'intimate moments' I shall gladly share with you, since you so insist, everything: boredom, anger, resentment, excruciating frustration, and ever more subtle realms of my hypocrisy and deceit until finally I've been ready on any number of occasions to murder him or myself or both of us" – he stabs the air as if with a knife – "yes! But just then one of *you* has shown up. Share it? You can have it all!"

John shifts his position but doesn't rise. No one looks at him.

"For awhile," he goes on, his voice softer, "I was waiting, it's true, hoping that, maybe *today* there will be real love between us. Thinking that he is only testing my faithfulness and, surely *today* . . . but as the todays wore on and on, something in my heart died, and I lost hold on hope." He sighs, then pauses for a long time.

"This terrible, aching loneliness began to grip me and – almost strangle me. . . . No, I can't possibly – describe . . . for awhile, I wondered if that first exaltation, that wrench into the light of love, really had anything to do with him, or if it had even really happened, or if he had played a trick with light.

"Now? Now I do nothing. I hardly even think. I certainly don't wonder why he is doing this any more, and what he means by this or that, or what or who he is. I don't believe or disbelieve. A procession is going on; I hang about the edges and play a part, but I'm not really in it. Not that I'm somewhere else. I . . .

"For awhile, too, I didn't know how I could keep on playing his 'favorite' for you all. But about then you began expecting me to be withdrawn in my 'devotion' – so there was nothing I had to do. Now I just continue on, letting the procession take me where it will.

"I can imagine what you're wondering now, so I also will make a confession; a good thing for a disciple to do. When I asked him tonight who the betrayer would be, he actually said this: 'The one to whom I give the bread.'"

The others murmur.

"But don't feel safe now. Don't think low of Judas and high of yourselves. Because Jesus said that to me

87

with the same look and tone of voice with which he has said, 'I love you with all my heart,' for these three empty years. But then he handed the bread to Judas with a look and tone of voice that reminded me of that first brilliant moment when he glanced at me, on the beach at Galilee. Judas looked back much as I wished I could have, and he seemed at last to feel what I wished I could have when I reached the Master's feet. But then when Judas rose to leave, for a flicker of an instant a frown – almost a scowl – came over his face. It was just when his face was turning past me; I don't know if Jesus or any of the rest of you could even have noticed it.

"So nothing's proved, nothing's certain. We're all right where we were a moment ago.

"But so what? If it becomes clear that I must kill my brother, or even him – so what? How bad can disgrace and damnation be? If I must be killed myself . . . what of it? How bad can the fires of hell be? How bad can 'extinction from the universe' be?"

John stops talking, then looks around at each of the others.

"There. I'm done. Is that what you wanted?"

No one looks at him. All are quiet.

Peter is still staring at his own feet. "John. . . . You know, he says that a kernel of wheat must fall to the ground and . . . die before – before it can . . . bring forth fruit."

John gazes at Peter. When he speaks, his voice

is soft. "Don't hold your breath, Peter."

"But John," Bartholomew pleads, "If – if this is the way you felt, why did you and James even bother to ask to sit by his side in the Kingdom of Heaven? Especially when you knew it would infuriate the rest of us."

John looks at James, bemused.

"James?" Bartholomew asks.

"James?" Philip echoes.

James squirms on his rock. "Actually . . . it was – at our mother's insistence. . . ." He laughs. "You know how mothers are."

Bartholomew turns back toward John. "*You* could have said that, John; we would have believed you. Especially knowing your mother. . . . "

John continues smiling at James. Bartholomew follows his glance.

" . . . unless you're saying there's more to it than that? James?"

James crosses his arms over his chest, then leans forward, elbows on his knees, eyes cast down. "Well, if you must know . . . it was not long after you and I had – uh – had had a discussion about the hierarchies in Heaven, Bartholomew. And that . . . set me thinking – "

Bartholomew stands and walks slowly, remembering. "You mean the time I argued we would all occupy high positions in Heaven, and you told me you thought I was being ridiculous?"

Philip laughs out loud.

Bartholomew continues. "But that was months ago. Odd that you should then turn around and grab for first place. . . . Hm! I wondered why I couldn't understand your doing that, and now I know. I thought perhaps John had persuaded *you* to ask Jesus about it with *him.*"

James does not reply.

Philip, smiling, faces John. "I still don't see why *you* got into that mess, John, given how you really see things around here."

"It was simple," John shrugs. "James and I had recently quarreled. When our mother insisted on this absurd request" – he snorts, shaking his head – "can you imagine? The two of *us*, sitting at his side forever in the Kingdom?" He laughs for a long time, then continues.

"Well, when she insisted, it seemed as good a way as any to patch things up so I wouldn't be bothered – though I'm sure that, if Jesus had granted that request – if he could've granted it! – we'd be bickering into eternity behind his back, in Heaven. But I knew the Master would refuse, and that you'd all find out, and *that* would provide a pretext for me to stop putting on such an elaborate show, and to withdraw a bit more. Which it did."

All are silent. Peter looks up and toward the rear, frowning. "What's that?"

Everyone is quiet, listening.

"It's – it's him!" Peter hisses. "He's walking back down the hill. He's coming back!"

In a weary, labored rush, each of the disciples assumes the position of prayer that he was in when their conversation first began. It is now night, and little light remains to illumine the clearing. Almost immediately the heads of two or three of the praying men begin to droop, and to bob. Soon it is too dim to see anything.

End of First Conversation

Second Conversation

T
he Apostles are clustered in the clearing in the Garden of Gethsemane. Most are situated as they were at the end of the First Conversation – in prayer, though some appear to be drifting if not altogether asleep. A nearly full moon has risen, and its light shines upon the clearing. Some of the Twelve are shivering, or huddling in their cloaks and shawls against the cold.

Thomas is looking for someone to talk to. He catches Philip's eye. "What happened?" he asks, in a loud whisper.

"I don't know," Philip replies, also whispering.

"We were all praying. The next thing we knew, he was waking us up and berating us."

"You noticed."

"Strange. But then, things are always strange around him."

"You noticed."

They cease talking. After a moment, Thomas opens his eyes, sits upright, stretches, looks about, and sighs. Some of the other Apostles also rouse themselves, without meeting one another's glances. Others continue in what appears to be fervent, silent prayer.

Thomas whispers a little more loudly, and to no one in particular. "Back again." He pauses, then turns to Philip once more. "Do you think he knew we'd been sitting here talking almost the whole time?"

"He's going to be crucified tomorrow," Philip says.

"I really don't think he even cares." He sighs.

"God. I wish Judas would get back. Maybe he knows what's going on around here."

Thomas nods. "At least he apparently knew what to do when the Master told him to do what he had to. If he said that to me, I wouldn't know whether to pray or piss."

He reflects for a moment, then grunts, gets up, and walks behind a tree.

Peter sighs for a long time, with a sound like the last cough of a dying beast. He rises from the attitude of prayer and starts pacing back and forth in the center of the clearing. Nothing is heard for a few moments but the thud of his footsteps.

"Death, death, death," Bartholomew intones. "All this talk of death tonight, of betrayal and being killed. I thought the Angel of Death was supposed to spare the Jews at the time of Passover. Why not us? Why not the Master?"

"Probably," Peter says, "because we're not Jews any more."

Andrew scoffs. "That's foolish. Of course we're Jews. And Jesus is said to be the greatest Jew of all time, the first and most beloved Son of the God of Israel."

Bartholomew is not persuaded. "But apparently that won't keep him from being killed very soon. And betrayed to his killers tonight."

"So, what do you think?" Peter asks them. "That,

in the days to come, the followers of his Church will at this time of year commemorate as Jews the passing over of the Angel of Death in Egypt long ago? Or that, as his disciples, they will mourn his voluntary death and celebrate his rising and ascending to the Father in these very days?"

"Already have it planned out, eh, Peter?" Philip smirks.

Peter glares at him.

"Maybe his followers will do both, Peter," James says. "*He* celebrated Passover tonight, and has all his life, each year."

Bartholomew interrupts. "No, he hasn't. Not when he was traveling in the East."

"Bartholomew, I've told you before," Peter snaps, "our Lord did not have to scour heathen lands for wisdom; he was born with it."

Bartholomew is not daunted. "Even so, where was he all those years no one knows about?"

James doesn't give Peter time to respond. "*As I was saying*, the Hebrew people were suffering a very real kind of death as slaves in Egypt – a death of their freedom under God – and the Passover celebrates our deliverance from that death and our rebirth as God's spiritual nation. Whereas Jesus often talks of having to endure this generation and this world, and he longs for his deliverance to the Father. So maybe the new Church, if it does separate from the old, will celebrate both."

Now Peter bristles. "James, for the last time, his Church must separate because he says that he is the cornerstone which the builders will reject. And it cannot celebrate the Hebrew Passover because the Hebrews' first-born sons in Egypt were spared, but the Son of God says he will not be spared, but will be killed – so that *we* may be spared punishment for our sins."

"But the Jews," James says, "have always borne the burden of the sins of all nations, before God, just as Jesus is now taking on the burden of the sins of all men. And in Egypt the Angel went out to kill not the oppressed but the oppressors. Jesus stands for the oppressed, and he is going to be killed . . . by – the oppressors . . . hm. That makes no sense."

"I agree," Peter says. "And the Lord implied the other night that the Jewish authorities will have a hand in his murder. And the lamb's blood on their doorposts will be *his blood,* which he is to shed on the cross. So that blood at their doors will no longer be a mark of innocence and deliverance. Henceforth, it will be a mark of guilt and damnation and punishment in the fires of hell. This generation will bear all the guilt for their own sins, for the blood of the innocent."

"Ugh!" Andrew makes a grimace. "Death, death, death; fire and death, indeed. Why is it called the Angel of Death? Why not the Devil?"

Peter regards his brother. "Death is not the devil's work; only murder is. The Lord says we all have to die so we can be born again from Spirit and baptized in the Holy Spirit. As men, we are all born from flesh in the water of the womb; but we must die to be born from something far greater, from 'the wind that blows where it wills.'"

"Whatever that means," Philip mutters.

No one speaks. Andrew bundles himself tighter. "Speaking of fire," he says, "I wish we had a little of the earthly variety right here."

"It's damp now, too," Thaddeus shivers. "It chills your bones."

Andrew nods. "That's because this spot is so low. All the mists collect here."

Thomas is stalking about in the background on the left. He belches.

"*Thomas*," Andrew pleads.

"What, do you think I'm faking now?" Thomas asks. "I tell you, that meal disagreed with me."

Silence.

"At least it's not wet here," Bartholomew observes. "The dust of the day's movement has settled, but not the dew of night. It is musty here, though; it smells of leaves and dead flowers. I guess the end isn't upon us yet; the figs have not begun to bud. Even the olives are bare. I wish the flowers would bloom again."

"I'd rather be here than in the city," says Matthew. "The whole place smells of burnt fat and entrails. But listen, if we want to be warm, why don't we huddle closer?"

Andrew and Bartholomew, shivering, move nearer Matthew. Thaddeus starts to, but instead only huddles tighter himself. The others mostly seem not to have heard. Matthew looks around at them all, exhaling. The three continue rubbing themselves as they lean against one another for warmth.

John has been looking away a long time, but apparently has had an ear for some of the discussion. "Talk about smells – I was just overwhelmed with a longing for the smell of the sea."

"We weren't at the shore so long ago," Matthew says.

Andrew shakes his head. "Only another fisherman could know what he means. It's not only the air. It's the smell of fish and water-soaked wood . . . of wet hemp nets drying on the shore and old rotting sea-soaked cloaks, and your own sweat drying on your skin under a desert-hot sun. And you're breathing deep and working hard and inhaling all that day after day, until, in a way, you *are* all that. Isn't that what you mean, John?"

John is still gazing into the distance. "Yes. I guess a whiff of sea breeze does evoke all that, though. What I was really longing for is to be there . . . you know?"

No one speaks. Matthew watches Peter pacing about. "Peter . . . you're getting on my nerves."

Peter sits again at the base of the great rock, but keeps on fidgeting.

Simon lumbers to his feet, stretching as he moves into the clearing. The mass of his body looms large over the others. He casts a bemused glance back at John. "I can feel, John, how an occasional whiff of sea might work into the heart of an old fisherman. Well, imagine what the constant smell of the land does to a farmer.

"Before I joined the Zealots, my family raised the best wheat in Galilee. And I'll tell you, those smells pull at me fiercely: the deep sharp odor of fresh turned soil, the green smell of the young shoots in summer, the rich brown gold aroma of the harvest. And not just smells. The sight of a man, loins girded, browned by sun and wind, bent to a plow or wielding a scythe. The crow of a cock – after so many years, I still sometimes leap up thinking of the wheat. When we're caught in the rain, I'm as like to consider its effect on the crop as I am to think of finding shelter." Simon pauses, contemplating. "I guess I've got farming in my bones."

"I know something of what you say," Philip says. "My family kept vineyards in Judaea. They weren't as good as my father claimed, but the work and the life was good enough to make it hard for me to see a vineyard or drink wine or even eat a grape, without a whole host of memories dragging me back."

Thomas is now lurking in the background on the right, behind the others. "My, my, such revelations!" he laughs. "Why have we never spoken of these things before? As for me, though seeing sheep and smelling them does bring 'hosts of memories' to my mind, I can't say I've *ever* wanted to do that work again. That was like slavery – filthy, mindless, and lonely."

"Mm," Matthew nods. "Understandable, Thomas. But, as for your question, it's not as if we've never spoken of all this. A few of us have, now and then, but always in low voices and briefly. I guess we all thought we could give ourselves to Jesus more fully without thinking and talking too much of the past." He sighs. "But it keeps creeping up on us, and it seems at the present we're too worn out to resist."

James snorts at him. "Don't glorify old memories, Matthew. As I recall, being a fisherman was a stinking, dirty, grueling life; slavery, as Thomas put it."

"That's because you always wanted to be a rabbi, isn't it, brother?" John is looking at James with a raised brow.

Simon moves forward. "James, it may have been hard, but I imagine it made you hard, too." He goes through the motions of what he describes, his words edged and taut. "Though I must admit I can't see how setting a sail and then floating on the wind can be any-thing like breaking one's back, row by row, on a plow; or how casting a net and waiting and then hauling it in can compare with swinging a scythe over and over, hour after hour, for days on end."

"Are you saying, farm boy, that being a fisherman is an easy lot?" Andrew grins.

Simon glowers down at him. "I'm saying it's easier than farming wheat, you pretty fish. And don't call me 'farm boy' unless you're prepared to show me that I am just that. In wrestling I wager I could break you in half quicker than the Master broke those fishes at Bethsaida – though," he laughs, "I won't guarantee you'll grow back as two scaly little Andrews."

"Whoa now!" Andrew backs away, laughing. "Certainly I'll take back 'farm boy.' Better call you 'ox,' as Matthew said! Besides, if you broke me in half right now, the stench would be unbearable."

"What?" John shouts. "We can't let this beast of burden slur the life of sail and net! I know a match for him." He turns toward Peter, who has been trying to pray. "Come, Simon Peter, out of your reveries now! We're calling on you to make Simon the Ox answer for his mouthings in a wrestling match!"

"What?" Peter looks at him aghast. "John, how can you indulge such a notion at a time like this? We should be praying for our souls, not wrestling one another!"

Matthew rolls his eyes heavenward. "Stop deceiving yourself, Peter. Have you been praying? No, you've been pacing and slapping your fist into your palm and working your mind into foam. Now why don't you come off your high perch and 'indulge' in a competition? You'll calm those nerves – and afterwards, you'll probably be better able to pray!"

Peter sighs and shakes his head. He looks down. "You're probably right. I've been feeling like I'd like to run and run until my legs and lungs collapse."

"So," Matthew retorts, "why not strain arm to arm with Simon here, until your guts break and your bones crack and your heart pumps bleeding blood? He's a match for you, I know that much."

"Nonsense," Peter snaps. "No one ever beat me at wrestling."

"*I* will." Simon's massive arms are folded across his chest.

"You really think so?" Peter stares at him. "Dear Lord," he says, eye to eye with Simon, "forgive me if I sin!"

"Hosanna to the heavens!" Philip shouts. "Simon the Rock versus Simon the Ox! And may the winner be crowned with laurel leaves, and receive eternal life!"

Peter and Simon move to a central table-like rock. Each gets down on one knee, elbows to the flat stone, still looking each other steadily in the eye. The others gather closer, except James, who stays on a rock on the left, and Matthew, who has been sitting near the center of the clearing all along.

Matthew assumes his role as referee. "Ready?" Everyone is still. Peter and Simon sit, eyes locked upon one another, bodies ready to explode in combat. "Begin!"

The two huge men strain mightily, but neither can budge the other. John shouts, "Stop playing, Peter!" and, to the others, "You watch, the Rock will flatten him in a minute." Philip rejoins, "Never! The Ox will bull him down in no time!" The others join in the cheering and pushing and baiting, except for Bartholomew, James, and James Alphaeus.

Bartholomew is tugging at Peter's cloak. "*Peter!* How can you do this? Brothers! This is no time for sport and games! *Stop it!*" He falls to the dirt. "Lord, forgive them!"

James Alphaeus leans toward the combatants and fans, shaking his fists and squinting with the effort of his words, as if shouting into a fiendish wind: "You know what he said? If the tenants don't respect the owner's son, the owner of the vineyard shall kill them! He'll find new tenants! Brothers, stop this blasphemy against the Lord, or *you'll be damned! As sure as this is night!*"

The wrestlers still make no headway against one another. Now each is beginning to tremble, muscles and veins about to burst out of their arms, necks, and faces.

After a time all the others become silent. The only sound is Peter's and Simon's breathing and grunting.

Finally, Matthew speaks. "Looks as if they will break a gut if they keep on. That's not a good idea tonight. As self-appointed judge, I call it a draw. You'd better stop now, brothers."

Peter and Simon disengage. Each collapses into the dirt, exhausted and gasping.

Speaking to no one in particular, John muses, "I could have sworn Peter would take Simon without a strain."

Simon puffs, "I'd've . . . destroyed him . . . three years ago – "

"Peter," Andrew laughs, "are you going to *take* that?"

Bartholomew is nearly in tears. "Peter, how could you *do* this?"

Peter doesn't look up. His head is hanging, and his arms barely hold his torso off the ground. When he speaks, his voice is rasping and tinged with horror. "What have I *done!* . . . what am I . . . doing? Master – my Lord! Forgive me!"

He hurls himself prostrate in the dust, weeping, praying, and gasping for air all at once. His hands clench fistfuls of dirt, then stretch toward the hill behind the clearing, where Jesus is praying.

Bartholomew and James Alphaeus immediately kneel in prayer. Matthew looks at them. Beads of sweat spring out on his scalp as he runs his fingers through wisps of hair. Soon he too is praying. Thaddeus also quickly sits down. Andrew and Thomas awkwardly pray on the edge of their boulders, where they had just been cheering.

The others look on or look away.

After a few moments Philip catches James's glance. "Matthew was right," he whispers. "It did help Peter's praying!"

James doesn't reply. The only sound now is Simon's belabored breathing.

Soon those at prayer begin to rouse themselves again, in nearly the reverse order of that in which they began. A couple of them stop, look to see who's still praying, and then return to prayer again for a few moments. James eventually turns to Philip.

"Peter *has* weakened. He used to be a brute, literally hard as a rock. He could have outwrestled Jacob himself back then, not to mention Simon. He *has* weakened."

"What do you expect," Philip says, "when all he's done for three years is walk all over the countryside, eating handouts, stolen corn, and stray figs, and exhausting himself every day? We're all much weaker men than we used to be."

John is listening. "You're right. About that, at least, there can be no doubt. I once felt strong and healthy in my body. Now it's like a soft, worn old rag. We're all sallow and gaunt. Not a one of us is what you'd call 'radiant' any more."

"Not even Jesus," Philip agrees. "He's like a bleaching skeleton these days. How long has it been since he's 'exuded power' to you, Simon?"

Simon is now recovered. "Physical strength? A long time. A *long* time."

No one speaks. After awhile Thomas saunters into the central open area and sits down near several of the others.

"I guess you're right," he says. "I didn't enjoy shepherding – I was lonely and I stank – but I felt better and I didn't worry about things I couldn't understand."

Andrew agrees. "Giving up your self is cruel and hard when a healthy body goes with it." He runs his fingers across his scalp. "Look at me: already losing my hair, and at my age!"

"It's not only hair and muscle," James says. "Our traditions, our homes, our friends, our families – we've given up everything, and those losses have weakened us, too."

Thomas scoffs. "*Most* of us have given up all that, James. Your brother John is here, and your old friends Peter and Andrew. Your mother follows Jesus and us around, and your father shows up every now and then to reclaim her. Most of us came alone and gave up all we had. It may not have been the Kingdom of Heaven, but it was still hard to part with."

"Was it really, Thomas?" Matthew asks.

"Yes! It was."

"I don't mean to challenge you," the older man says. "It just hasn't been that hard on me. I've found it almost too easy; like throwing away a ragged, smelly old cloak and putting on something fine and new."

Simon, walking back to his rock near John, stops to look at Matthew with a baleful stare. "Of course, Matthew, yours was a despicably smelly old cloak."

Thomas smiles. "And that's what keeps 'creeping up on you,' as you put it earlier?"

"No, only the pleasant patches remain," Philip adds, "and though they don't match your new cloak, as you said even earlier, Matthew, you still haven't thrown them out – "

"*Whatever* the case," Matthew exhales, looking at Thomas and Philip, "for me there was little of this pain from leaving my previous life. When the Master smiled and said, 'Follow me,' all the worry and self-hatred was lifted off my shoulders like a mountain of refuse, and flung away."

Simon glares at him from behind. "If you hated it, Matthew, why did you have to wait for Jesus?"

Without turning toward Simon, Matthew draws slow, uncertain circles in the dust with a finger. "Because . . . it was a difficult situation to leave, Simon. I had no friends, no family, there was no other work I could do. And on the other side, the authorities don't take lightly to someone's leaving. You think we were their 'collaborators,' that we enjoyed the spoils with them. You're *wrong* on that, Simon. Like all the other Jews, tax-gatherers are *slaves* to the Romans. Only the game is subtler. Because their work earns tax-gatherers the utter hatred of their own people, the Romans have to play on their vanities and vices to keep them faithful. Once tax collectors have earned reputations as pigs among the people, and the Romans know it, then they no longer pretend to favor them. Then the poor fools are caught in the vise of their own greed. And from then on, the Romans rule them with sheer terror and force, the same way I imagine they do in the mines."

Matthew pauses, as if listening to himself, then lets out a hard laugh. *"Mines!* The same way they do in the *towns*, the same way they rule in our fields all over the land. It's not as blatant out in the open, perhaps, but it's just as effective. A few simple principles of oppression and exploitation applied through firm policies and tactics, which must vary here and there according to local conditions. That much I learned as a tax-gatherer. Tyranny operates very simply."

Peter has stopped praying and is listening from the ground. His voice is still and soft, but firm again. "Brothers, can we still not stop all this loose talk and complaining? Tyranny must not operate so well on the shore of Galilee, Matthew. I never met a Roman or a tax-gatherer – or a Pharisee – who attempted to take extortions from *me*, or to steal my fish. Or my father's. Taxes were high, but not intolerable. I felt they had no right to rule us, but their rule did not seem tyrannical."

Simon is incensed. "Because they have no right to rule, the rule itself *is* tyranny!"

Peter sighs and returns to his spot on the base of the large boulder. John watches, waiting for him to resume his seat. "How long has it been since you've heard from your father, Peter? And you can't deny the stories some of the others told about what happened to them."

Philip's eyes are flashing. "Yes, you must have met some rare Romans, Peter, or scared them off with your rock-hard, petrified muscle. Obviously you've never seen your vineyard burnt and your sister raped by drunken Romans, while you were held with a spear at your throat."

All are silent. A few look toward Philip. Matthew speaks. "Did that happen to you, Philip?"

Philip, standing and leaning against his tree, looks down and away.

Then James Alphaeus bursts out: "It wouldn't have happened to them and to you, Philip, if you hadn't called it down upon yourselves. That is the vengeance of the Lord of Hosts! I know that's the truth of it. And you'd better not deny or blaspheme against the wrath of God!"

Smoldering, Philip turns and walks slowly toward James Alphaeus, who does not move from the ground in front of Peter. *"You know nothing!"* Philip can barely contain his rage. "I may have become wicked, but that was only later. And my sister was *innocent* right up till the moment she died of their pleasures." He grasps James Alphaeus and lifts him by the neck of his cloak. "You and your contemptuous curses – you're a blasphemer against *life*, you terrified little – "

"Philip. . . ." Peter's word visibly affects Philip, as if harnessing his fury. But Philip keeps his eyes on James Alphaeus as he continues to berate him. "Hah!" he sneers. "You all call *me* 'dark at the mouth'? Listen, you ass, I'll forgive you this insult because you're such a stupid fool!" He throws James Alphaeus down again. "Such a frightened idiot!"

Still bristling, Philip walks away from James Alphaeus – then turns back toward him, barely able to restrain himself.

"But from now on, you'd better spare me your threats and imprecations! When your mighty Lord Jesus told a man his sins were forgiven, the man leapt with joy, but the Pharisees muttered, 'Blasphemy, blasphemy!' Now I say my family was tyrannized by the Romans, plain facts, and you dare to call *that* blasphemy? *How dare you!* You call everything blasphemy. All you think about is blasphemy and transgression! Fear and evil! Satan and damnation! Listen, Alphaeus: Don't talk to me any more until you crawl out of your cave, or your pit, or whatever it is you're in. Because I don't want to hear that shit – and I won't hear it, I'm warning you!"

"Easy, Philip," Matthew says.

Philip returns to a seat under his tree. He can't stop fuming.

Andrew turns to James Alphaeus. "You know, he's right, James. You never say a word of love or joy. You're always condemning and cursing and threatening – even after Jesus chastised you."

James Alphaeus responds instantly, in a very loud voice. "A man has to speak up for what he sees as the truth. As I see it, Jesus chastised me for cursing the already damned, whom it's *his* job to curse. I must watch out for my own brothers. I don't think most of us are any more aware than the Pharisees of how close we stand to the edge of the pit, even now, or of how terrible damnation is."

He looks down, but his voice still rings out. "I cannot make jokes. I am not at ease in loose talk. I have tried, but I can't do it. I am always watching out. And I feel that because of that, you all have never really accepted me as your brother." He looks up. "Even you, Peter. I have always been alone among you."

Grim-lipped, James Alphaeus bows his head. Philip sneers and snorts.

Thaddeus points, almost lunges at Philip. "Don't you think that, Philip!" He sits back, flushed. "He's not just making that up or pitying himself. I've – often felt the same way among you. Always being put down and brushed off; out on the edges and – and almost . . . unnecessary. Not even needed. A waste of everyone's time."

"Thaddeus," Bartholomew murmurs, "I'm sure we all feel that way at one time or another."

"But not most of the time!" Thaddeus shouts. "Not all the time! Not *right now!*"

James Alphaeus clears his throat, waiting for the others' attention. "Still," he says firmly, "that is no cause for a man to shirk doing what he sees as the Lord's will. I try to treat you as my brothers, even if you don't accept me. And if I see one of my own brothers playing about on the edge of hell, I must speak up, and I must speak strongly! With the Master's own words! Tonight we are flirting with damnation as never before. I *had* to say that to Philip just now – and I would not have said it so strongly if the same and worse had not happened to me."

He pauses, looking around at the other Apostles. "My father was a merchant in Jerusalem. He began to make deals with the Romans, cheating the poor. Now I don't say the Romans are the arm of the Lord, Philip; they're the arm of Satan, evil itself. But then my father tried to cheat the Romans. And just as the Lord God in all His power has used the wicked to chastise the wayward children of Israel since the days of our fathers, so the Lord God struck down my father and his family for his wickedness. The Romans came in the night, killed my father, stole my mother and sisters away for slaves and concubines, and beat me near to death.

"So I say to you with certainty, Philip, that someone in your family brought the jealous wrath and terrible will of the Lord of Hosts down upon you!"

Philip leaps up in rage. James Alphaeus scrambles over a rock and darts behind a tree, where he stands intent and unblinking, like a mouse dodging a cat. Philip shakes his fist.

"I warned you, you – you *scorpion!*" he shouts, trembling. "You *lizard!* I'll beat you *all* the way to death if you don't shut up!"

"*You* shut up, Philip, and *sit down.*" Peter barely stirs, his words quiet but fierce. He is sitting within an arm's reach of Philip. They stare at each other for an instant, then Philip whirls and returns to the tree on the right. His eyes continue to betray his fury for a long time.

"And you, James Alphaeus," Peter continues, "perhaps you'd best stick to looking after yourself. We owe you – and you, Thaddeus – a great debt of love. Others of us have spurned or ignored what you tried to give of yourselves. By his grace, hopefully, you have become stronger because of it. Please forgive us all.

"But James Alphaeus, you had better remember the Master's words about attending to the plank in your own eye rather than the speck in your brother's. If you must judge, despite what he said about judging, keep it to yourself. We don't want to hear it. And, I assure you, we *won't.*"

James Alphaeus quails before Peter and, still tight-lipped, looks down. Simon has been listening with increasing agitation. Now his words rumble out of him like an avalanche.

"That's well and good for his judging Philip, but don't try, Peter, to extend it to our fight with the Romans. And Matthew! My question: You say you couldn't leave tax-gathering because you had no friends and knew no other work. Why couldn't you have joined the Zealots? With your knowledge, you could have done great work for the movement."

Matthew, finger in the dirt, draws one good, firm circle. "I was *afraid*, Simon. I admit it. And if I had joined them . . . why, that would be the worst thing a tax-collector could do for the cause of freedom."

He looks into the eyes of his accuser. "Your people don't realize: They're just playing with you now, Simon. But if a few tax-gatherers were to join you, or some other significant 'collaborators,' the Romans would unleash a whirlwind upon you. If a good number of their slave 'officials' joined you, you'd be done for. And not because they'd be afraid of state secrets getting out. *Knowledge?* Simon, we didn't know a damned thing. *I* didn't. But they'd devour your freedom fighters, not out of fear, but because of another weakness: They're very jealous about their own slaves."

"Things will change," Simon spits, "only when people dare to sacrifice themselves, Matthew. The Zealots are not afraid to die. They don't fear their movement's destruction, either. You could have found a way, if you had tried." He stares at Matthew.

Philip has been brooding and pacing in the foreground of the clearing. "Oh, stop bothering him, Simon!" he says. "Why do you persist in begrudging him his past?"

"What about you, Philip?" Simon retorts. "You yourself say the Romans are tyrants and brutes. Why didn't you work for liberation with the Zealots after you left your burnt vineyards, instead of chasing after whores and wine?"

"Because the Zealots," Philip snarls, gesticulating, "are nothing more than a gang of power-seeking cutthroats, that's why! With their quick little daggers, murdering anyone who gets out of their narrow line. Simon, the people may cheer Zealot petty heroics, but they'll never rise under their leadership. Zealots would be worse tyrants than Romans, because they're neither as cunning nor as cosmopolitan. So I was just as much caught in a vise as Matthew."

"'Let's not fight, brothers," Thomas teases. He looks at Matthew. "But, you know, you still haven't told us one thing – how did you ever get such a rotten job, anyway? You didn't apprentice for it, did you?"

Matthew laughs. "No, no . . . ah . . . " – he looks at his feet in the dust – "I really don't wish to speak about that."

"Come, come, Matthew," Thomas says, rolling his eyes. "You're likely to be dead or condemned by dawn, or swallowed up in the end of time. Come, there's no room for secrets among brothers, right?"

Simon turns away and picks up his stick and his thoughts again. Matthew considers what Thomas has said.

"Yes," he replies, earnestly, after a pause. "You're right. Because I believe that, Thomas, and because I want you also to really believe it, I'll tell you. I've never told anyone before. I'll tell you as my brothers."

He hesitates, struggling to get words out. "My . . . mother – was a . . . concubine. For a particularly evil-minded Roman procurator. He noticed my early talents in mathematics, promised me an education in Rome, but sent me here instead where I was pressed into service by one of his friends. His own . . . son."

He can't go on for a moment. No one else speaks.

"I thank the Lord my mother was a Jewess."

Thaddeus is whispering. "Why didn't you run away *then?*"

Matthew slides from his rock to the ground, sighing. "You're wearing me to a nub. Where could I have run to?" His face clouds as he looks at Simon and Thomas. "I tell you," he shouts, "you're all such naive little fools! *You have not taken the measure of these men!*"

Matthew's rage dissipates and is gone. He sighs again. "Besides, I was greedy and spiteful. I have plenty of my father in me, too. And . . . they did make nice promises."

"Mm," Philip says. "The land of milk and honey."

Matthew nods. "So you can see why I have few regrets about being here. Jesus – and you all – are everything to me. And dear God, I don't want to betray him." He is quiet.

Simon tap, tap, taps with his stick.

Matthew runs his fingers through his hair and goes on. "I'm very tired of betrayal. Forgive me my doubts and my crude sinful heart, but don't make me betray him. I've got to admit, I hope it's someone else who's got that fate to face."

"So do we all," Thomas sneers. *"Brothers."*

There is a long silence. Philip clambers around

Peter to the top of the massive rock and stands looking up to the rear.

"Why doesn't he come down off that hill again? I've never seen anybody pray so long." He turns and jumps down, nearly losing his balance and then righting himself. "And *why* doesn't Judas come back? He'd probably have the gall to admit it, if he were plotting."

Simon tap, tap, taps.

Andrew laughs and rubs himself. "Jesus Judas Judas Jesus Jesus. Yes, he never lacked for gall. What was his early life like, anyway? Anyone know? Or is it also clouded in mystery?"

"I know a little," Thomas says. "He was born in a Judean town and was very devout as a boy. His father was a priest. Hm – it's the same story, practically. A Roman officer began blackmailing his father over something. When Judas found out, he lost faith completely. Because his father was giving this Roman everything the family owned and was even stealing from the Temple to protect himself."

Simon takes up a regular, slow rhythm, knocking more loudly with each strike. Thomas continues.

"Judas told his father either to confess to the people or say goodbye to his only son. His father cried on his knees before him. Judas left and became completely wicked until he met Jesus. Even then, it was a long time before he found new faith in the Father, and much longer before he began to believe in Jesus as the Son . . . hm. The old thug. Now that I think of it, Judas is like the way-ward son in the parable, returned now to his true Father. I wonder if Jesus is the jealous elder brother."

"Thomas!" Peter snaps.

"I was just wondering," Thomas says.

"Well, you shouldn't!" Peter is exasperated but his voice is tired, his words tinged as much with duty as with indignation. "If we accept what you say, Judas at least has now found faith in Jesus as the Messiah, not as a mortal human brother. If that is true, then *Judas* would know that the divine Son knows no jealousy, nor any other crude passion."

Thomas doesn't lower his eyes but doesn't reply. Simon's tapping becomes quite loud.

James makes a forced laugh. "The Master really picked a band of saints, didn't he? Matthew's taxes and wine, Judas a thug, me with ambitions to be a Temple authority, Philip with his women, John with *his* – "

"Don't say that," John cuts in. "That's not the truth." He is still looking off into the distance. The others turn toward him, startled.

"Now, John," James says, "when someone plays around, people know. It wasn't something you could hide."

"But that wasn't whoring. It was real." Now John turns to face them all. "That was love. I was really in love, with every one of them. You laugh! It was like 'The Song of Songs.' You bastards don't know what love is!"

Simon taps a few more times. Matthew yells, "Simon . . . *must you?*"

Simon shrugs and drops the stick as James speaks again.

"Quite a thing for you to say at this point, John."

"But it's true," John says, his voice rising. "I may have forgotten but you never knew, James!"

"Don't get angry, John," Andrew says. "But – shouldn't just one woman have sufficed, if you were truly in love with her? And why did you never marry?"

John's smile does not lessen the rage in his eyes. He shrugs. "If Jesus 'loves' everyone, why can't I? No, seriously, I . . . I guess I was always longing for someone even more beautiful, more tender-hearted, more perfect . . . no. That's not really right. They *were* perfect, each in herself."

He stops to reflect, then looks back up, his eyes fiery again. "But listen! I don't have to answer your questions! Of course there were moments of mere infatuation, and times when I exploited women who desired me. I'm not perfect. But *many* were the moments when I and a woman dwelt in love, and it was for them I always sought. That was love; I know it in my heart, and your questionings mean nothing."

John stands and walks near the trees on the western side of the clearing. His motions are fluid and graceful, and when he speaks again, all stress has left his voice.

"Have you ever felt with a woman that your soul

and hers were like two streams flowing together to form a single river, the currents playing off and merging in one another all the way downstream? Makes you breathless with wonder, I can tell you. Have you ever come to realize that no matter what you do, your lover will respond with a movement or word that just complements yours, and you will do the same for her? And that even your arguments are dances? Love is not rutting, or being sweet to one another, or making a marriage arrangement. It is like an airy garden at the top of a steep hill, where you can stand and look down upon the desert wilderness, and the plains dotted with herdsmen and their flocks, and the busy towns of men below. And in that garden two souls can meet and embrace and commingle and sing and dance, argue and hurt, turn away and turn back, in an eternity of perfect moments – "

He pauses to gaze at several of the others. "Your eyes tell me you think I exaggerate. All right – certainly not all the moments are perfect. For one thing, you must struggle to get to that place – though when you finally arrive, it seems as if you've been picked up, as if by a great bird or a hand, and just dropped there. But then you may find your beloved is not there. And then you may wonder if you're really there yourself. And you may stumble and fall back down the hillside. If the two people are not perfect, how can their love be perfect? But after one such moment, in that place, you wait and watch and yearn breathlessly for the next, and the next, and the next.

You seek an endless string, a necklace of them.

"No, say what you like about me and my 'women,' you'll never persuade me I didn't live in love with them and always seek to love them more."

Matthew ponders, then replies. "I didn't think you were exaggerating. But if you had found this kind of love with women, John . . . why have you stayed so long with the Master?"

John shrugs, sits, and looks away.

"John, you may persuade *yourself*, but you'll never again persuade me that you're not yearning for the Master's love even now." Matthew is surprised by the revelation of his own words. "Because you met *him* at the gate of that garden once, but he wouldn't let you in. It's *his* garden! Maybe he's keeping you out so that when you do get in you'll never ever leave again! . . . You're dying for his love, even now. Because his Spirit to your soul is like Galilee to a stream, to the Jordan. . . . He calls us friends of the Bridegroom, but – you . . . you may deny it, but you *are* more like a bride! You're *dying* for his love, John! And the only reason you act differently is because it's easier to pretend you're already dead and the pain is over."

John doesn't look at Matthew. "That's not true. I remember all that, but I don't feel it any more. I don't."

Matthew rises heavily, as if weighted with age. He strides slowly to John, and gently turns John's face toward his own.

"Face it, John, face it. Those words you just spoke could not have come from an indifferent, barren heart. Maybe from an empty heart; but an empty heart is a heart dying with yearning for fullness. And you know *that* in your heart."

John turns away.

"'Be perfect, even as my Father in Heaven' . . . " Andrew muses. "Hmm. To attract John with such an unspoken promise of love, and then to take it away and torment him all these years? Will he ever fulfill the promise . . . ?"

"He's taking everything away from everyone," James says, his words clipped. "Isn't it obvious? Look at us. Whatever anyone clings to or wants the most, Jesus is taking or keeping it away from him. John and John's love. Thomas and *his* love, his belief. Peter's faith and loyalty. Matthew's new family here, disintegrating before our eyes. My understanding – "

"James, please, no more talk," Bartholomew begs, wearily. "Haven't we talked enough?"

James cuts him off. "You may have; I have not." He looks away for awhile. "I thought the Covenant guaranteed a face-to-face relationship between man and God. But Jesus says we're doomed if we have no faith in *him*. 'I am the Way, the Truth, and the Life.' 'No one can come to the Father except through me.'"

James begin pacing, with measured steps. His voice is clear and strong but he's thinking out loud, addressing no one other than himself.

"The Lord God Himself has always said that He alone is the Bridegroom and Shepherd of Israel. Now Jesus comes claiming those roles for himself. He is usurping our common faith in the One of Whom it is said, 'Hear, O Israel, the Lord your God, the Lord is One.' No wonder they accuse him of blasphemy. . . .

"In the beginning, at least, he spoke mostly of the Father; but now he talks about himself. 'Ask in my name, and you shall receive.' We were never even allowed to *say* the Father's Name, much less to use it for this or that."

Some of the others listen now and again to what James is saying. Most do not.

"He calls the Lord his 'Father,' but every now and then he'll deliberately address someone as 'my son.' Or, 'my daughter,' as he said to the Samaritan woman at the well in Sychar. A woman, a heathen Samaritan, with many 'husbands' besides. Consorting with Jewish prostitutes is enough; but calling heathen whores 'my daughter'?"

Philip interrupts. "What have you got against heathen and whores, James? Jesus wants to save everyone, not just pious Jews."

James either doesn't hear Philip, or ignores him. "The Lord God said, 'Honor your father and mother,' and Jesus has spoken of it to the Pharisees. But he also says children must hate parents and brothers and sisters if they want to be disciples of his."

"But he doesn't really mean 'hate,' James," says Matthew. "He wants us to love everyone. He probably means you should love him more than you love them."

James is now moving more quickly. "It's still a source of terrible division. Most of our own families have been torn apart by our new lives. Look at his family – he won't even speak to his own mother, who suckled him at her breast. The only father he recognizes is God. He won't set foot in his own house or town. 'Leave the dead to bury their dead,' he says, 'if you want to follow me.' The only family he recognizes is his disciples. But none of us will ever have a real family again; we'll never be blessed with children to teach and raise in the ways of our fathers. We'll never 'be fruitful and multiply.' Abraham, Isaac, and Jacob did not have to leave their families to enter the Kingdom of Heaven. The family – the living core of our people's life – he's ripping it apart."

Philip, muttering under his breath, crosses the clearing from the right to the far left. James, a few feet away, is slumping to the base of a tree. Several of the others are in prayer. James continues.

"It's no secret he's destroying the Sabbath as well, and that he's making the Law secondary to his own teachings. And not all the rabbis and Pharisees are malicious men . . . many have spent their lives in earnest study, trying to understand God's Word. Many had come to think the Messiah would never really come, but that the Lord nonetheless requires us to live our lives in the Law, expecting him every moment. Or that if he did come, certainly he would come confirming the Law, not setting it aside. So you can imagine how Jesus impresses them. The *Law! God's Commandments!* The foundation of our nation! I swear it, Jesus is tearing Israel apart at the roots, destroying all the things that have united our people since the days of Abraham himself."

Peter is listening from his rock. "You're ranting, James; control yourself. Our Lord knows what we have abandoned for him. He has said, 'In very truth I tell you this: There is no one who has given up home, or family, or belongings, who will not be repaid many times over in this age, and in the age to come have eternal life.' Did not the Father Himself tear all that away from our ancestor Job? But Job remained strong in faith, and the Lord rewarded him a hundredfold at the end of his days."

While Peter goes on, Thomas, ever roaming, wanders around and meets Philip in the bushes on the left, just beyond the space in the clearing where most of the others are sitting. They whisper for a moment, then Thomas faces Philip, clasps his hands palm to palm as if to pray, and holds them straight out in front of him.

Philip squares off, hands to his side, and suddenly slaps at Thomas's with his right. Thomas lifts both hands; Philip misses, and it is now Thomas's turn. The game is slow at the start – they keep missing or nearly missing. A couple of trees partially obscure them from view.

"As for the rest of what you say," Peter is continuing, "the Law may be the foundation, James, but Christ completes it; more, he is its cornerstone. And look, he himself has said, 'I have come to bring a sword, not peace.' He has to cut away old weeds to make way for a sturdy new tree, the coming age. It's his sword that's at work among the people, not for his benefit but for theirs; and it's at work among us tonight, cutting deep into every heart and mind."

Simon leaps to his feet just as Thomas lands a good hit.

"I *disagree* with every word you say! The *Romans* had taken away all those things long before Jesus arrived. Our relationship to God – look at Judas's father, a priest bribed by infidels. The Law – Alphaeus the elder, cheating the poor and playing housedog for Caesar. Our families – Matthew's mother, a paid whore. The Sabbath – money-changers in the Temple, working with Rome. And you know all these things have been happening all across the Land ever since the occupation began."

Philip connects as Simon talks on. "Israel is nearly destroyed already. Jesus is talking about a sword for liberation and new unity, not a sword to destroy what little unity we have left."

"*Nonsense*." Peter is equally strident. "Worldly *madness*. Do you think he wants to establish an earthly kingdom? You want him to be a worldly leader, when you know very well that the Devil took him to a mountaintop and tempted him, showing him all the nations of the world in a vision, and he rejected the demon's offer? If you want that, *you're* a devil, Simon!"

Thomas hits Philip hard, three times in succession. Peter is oblivious to them as he continues. "His sword is destroying all that's left of Israel now – weeds and refuse. Rome could not make God's people turn against him if they did not want to. Rome is only exploiting our own wickedness; and Jesus is not concerned about such a trifle as Rome. He's concerned not with national freedom, but with spiritual freedom. What good is a nation's freedom – and even outward peace – if the people's minds are bound by darkness and their hearts seethe with violence?

"Our Master is speaking only of, and leading us only to, the inner salvation of each soul. Not external liberation. There is no such thing, without the Spirit. You can't have listened to him 'with ears that hear,' Simon, and still be able to deny that."

Thomas whispers, loud enough to be heard by all, "Here we go again. Simon the Rock versus Simon the Ox."

Philip hits him a loud slap. "Pay attention, little one."

"I don't deny that, Peter," Simon says, walking about. "But he is also speaking about the liberation of the soul of our people, our nation – else how can he be the promised Messiah of Israel? And he *does* speak of overthrowing oppressive power and wealth, and not just Rome's – like the power of the doctors of the Law who 'eat up the property of widows.' He's always talking about overthrowing. 'The first shall be last, and the last first.'"

Peter lets out a laugh. "Surely you don't believe he means that about any place but the Kingdom of *Heaven*? Surely you don't, Simon! And what about what he said to the Pharisees just the other day?" Peter pauses; Thomas lands a vicious hit; Peter goes on. "'Render unto Caesar that which is Caesar's, and unto God that which is God's.' *That* was *clearly* supporting Caesar's worldly authority, wasn't it?"

Philip yelps, "Ai! Son of a – " just as Simon lunges to his feet with a half-throttled roar.

"*Damn it*, Peter!" he rages. "How can you be so blind? Don't you know that the whole thrust of the liberation movement is *based* on the fact that *Israel* is God's, not Caesar's? Haven't you heard the Zealots saying for years that Israel should bow before no man, much less a swine in Rome? Or do you actually think Jesus was talking about a handful of coins? He was talking about *the life blood and soul of our people*, which we've been giving to these heathen Romans more freely than we give money to beggars – or to the Temple, even.

"And don't think his meaning was lost on those Pharisee vultures, either!"

Philip connects, four times, hard.

"They know he wasn't talking about a few taxes but about their fat and plunder-swollen lives. Alas for them is right! Because when the Romans are overthrown, they will be back in the streets – if they succeed in begging for their lives – and all their spoils will be returned to the ones it was stolen from, the people."

Simon is ranting now, bolting about, sometimes nearly smacking into the others. They all try to give him as much room as they can.

"And what about those coins with that tyrant's head on them? Can you be so blind that you did not see it? If he had said anything against Caesar, they would have arrested him immediately! So he said pay Caesar what you owe him, and pay God what you owe *Him*. But the truth is, the Jewish people don't owe Caesar a damn penny!"

Thomas, quicker than Philip, hits him six times.

"Because the Romans invaded our Land which was given to us in covenant with the Lord God Himself, and now they're taxing us as if we were *their tenants*. But we're *God's* tenants, and we owe Caesar nothing but his own downfall! *And we owe that to God as well: Caesar's downfall!*"

"Shh!" Thaddeus hisses. "Not so loud, Simon; the soldiers are about, they'll hear you."

Simon slumps onto a rock and folds his arms. "I don't care. I might as well be arrested, at this point. Three years I've been waiting for the real struggle to begin, but there's been nothing but talk. I've gone back over it all tonight. *Three years!* And now he speaks out so plainly against Caesar as that – and in the next moment he says he's giving himself up to them.

"Hell, I might as well betray him myself. He's betrayed me. I joined him because I saw in him a great leader of our people, a David who could slay a thousand Goliaths."

Philip scores; Thomas shakes his hand and moans. Simon is oblivious to their noise.

"And now at the very moment when the people are all united behind him, and the Romans and their fat collaborators are scared shitless of him – he gives dire mystic warnings and says he's giving himself up to them to be killed. I just don't see it. Not at all."

Thomas is scoring one sharp hit after another.

Thaddeus says, "Perhaps he means both an 'inner sword' and and an 'outer sword.' Perhaps he's going to perform a miracle and drive out the Romans after he's risen from the dead, Simon."

Simon leaps up again. "Of course he means both! *What about those swords* over there, Peter?" He rushes to the swords leaning against a tree and brandishes one. "What about what he said just before we came in here? How could I have forgotten – how could I have forgotten it till now?! 'It's different now,' he said. No more going barefoot. We are to take our purses and packs. He told us to sell our cloaks to buy *swords!* Lilies of the field, indeed! He recited from Scripture – he's to be counted among *outlaws*. Maybe he still means to lead the insurrection and rule our Land!"

Thomas misses. Philip begins to connect, more slowly than Thomas, but more powerfully, time after time.

Peter has not risen or moved. He shouts back at Simon, "*Nonsense!* He may mean that Israel should free herself from the Romans, and I don't know what we are supposed to do with those swords – but he certainly *will not* be leading any insurrection himself! The Devil already offered him the whole world, *but he refused it!* Don't you understand that yet? He told us he's to be counted among outlaws, spat upon, and *killed*. And in three days he will rise again, but only to make himself known to us and to ascend to the Father. *Not to lead insurrections*, Simon!

"And Philip! Would you two please *stop playing games?!*"

Philip whispers to Thomas, "I'm ready to quit, anyway."

Thomas is nearly on his knees. "Me too."

As Peter continues, Philip smiles and tousles Thomas's hair – then yelps as Thomas dodges away and slaps his hand one last time. Thomas grins. They sit down in the bushes, where they listen and sometimes laugh and whisper.

"And we owe God nothing, Simon," Peter is saying, "but all the love of our heart and mind and strength. That is the First Commandment of God Himself. We owe Caesar nothing but the same love we pay ourselves. Love your neighbor as your own self, the

Master says; or, if you prefer to put it another way, then love your enemy and pray for your persecutor. And if he strikes you, Simon, turn the other cheek."

Matthew has been shaking his head. "That's all true and good, Peter, in principle; but look at the actual realities. How could Judas's father have turned wholly to God without being destroyed? How could my mother love God or man while a paid slave of the Romans? How could I have turned my life to God, if I had not met Jesus?"

"Precisely." Peter nods with vigor. "Jesus is the Way. He does not make life easy. He has promised us further persecutions and oppressions; yet we must 'fear not those who kill the body, but fear the One who can kill body and soul.' All he requires is faith in him and love of God and man – nothing more. All the other rules and laws pale in significance before these, Matthew – and you too, James: for if we do these with every shred of our energy, how can we fail to please the Lord by our acts? Then, in truth, we will be able to do no wrong."

Matthew and James do not meet Peter's glance. He continues, with ardent whispers.

"And what does he promise we shall receive for our efforts? Eternal life! A life which lasts forever, in which each moment will be so glorious and full that whole lifetimes of this life seem like death, by comparison! The Kingdom of Heaven! The true Land of Milk and Honey! *Paradise unimaginable and everlasting!* How can any earthly freedom compare with that?

"Listen – man will not free Israel from Rome. God will, and in His own time. About that, it is *not* different now: Tomorrow is still not ours to worry or strive about. Our only concern should be to lay ourselves body, mind, and soul at our Lord's feet right now."

Like lightning, Simon slashes two branches off an olive tree near the center of the clearing. James Alphaeus and Bartholomew are within inches of his flashing sword. James Alphaeus ducks aside, but Bartholomew seems not to notice.

"Peter," Simon bristles, brandishing the sword, "listen to me, and listen well for once, 'if you have ears to hear.' *What you have said makes no sense to me*. For me to have real faith in God is to work for justice in his name. That's why I left my farm. For me to lay myself body, mind, and soul at the Lord's feet – and *not* at Jesus's feet, for to me he is a great man but only a man. I will not prostrate myself before Caesar, and I will not prostrate myself before Jesus. I'll sit in my Master's lap, yes, and I will give my life to my people's leader – but I will not lay myself down to him as the Lord. I'm too much a Zealot. I prostrate myself before God in Heaven alone! And for me to do that means not to lie down, but to stand upright, gird my loins, and fight for the restoration of justice and mercy – and love – in His own chosen Land, His Kingdom of the Earth, among His own chosen people. As our fathers stood and fought in days gone by."

He glares at Peter, who glares back. Neither moves.

"Otherwise, what you say is mere words to me, Peter. I am not a man of words. I can speak with words, but I cannot pray with words. You stand with Jesus's words, James stands with the Law and the prophets. But for me to try to stand before the face of God with words would be like trying to make the Jordan run backwards from the sea to the mountains. It can't be done. And if it could, it would be to no purpose.

"I must pray with *action*, with movement, with change; I must pray with energy spent in God's service, in God's will, and for His justice and glory! One moment of real service to God and His people can give me all the joy and fullness I could ever desire. I seek fulfillment in this life, not eternal life. In this world, not in paradise. The *real* Promised Land will be a liberated Israel.

"And listen: If He had wanted me different, wouldn't He have made me so?"

Simon sits wearily, the sword falling from his hand and clattering onto the ground. "So don't try to make me like you, Peter. All right: I admit it, the Zealots have become murderers. That's why I left them for Jesus; he didn't have to tell me their ways were no longer mine. And I admit I have been overlooking some of what Jesus has taught us, because it doesn't fit my ways. I don't know what to do about it. And this constant waiting and helpless watching is killing me. I rage in one moment and stagnate the next. At least I knew some real service with the Zealots. Now, watching precious moments slip by, watching this greatest and most noble leader throw himself away, destroy himself – you just don't know how it eats at my heart. You don't know how it gnaws at my very soul."

Silence. Peter ponders, biting his lip. It is getting darker now.

"Simon," Peter ventures after a while, "I still cannot help but wonder, if you do not have faith in Jesus as the Christ and Son of God, and do not want that faith in him . . . then what are you doing here?"

Simon sighs with a cough, his throat rattling. "Nothing, Peter. Precisely nothing."

No one speaks. Simon, brooding, suddenly sniffs. "All right. Who farted?"

"I did," Matthew says, a sheepish smile on his lips. "My guts are like surf tonight, all wind and waves."

"Foul wind, that's for sure. I hope you'll spare us the waves."

"I'll try, Simon. But it could have been anyone, you know. You too. We've all been stifling belches and quieting farts all night."

Once again no one has anything to say. Bartholomew looks up through the branches of the trees into the night sky. He appears to be searching for something in the heavens. Eventually, heaving an exhalation, he lowers his gaze and closes his eyes, either in prayer or in exhaustion. Matthew and Andrew are shivering in the chill of the night. Philip gets up and walks around behind the boulder to his tree on the western edge of the open space.

Thomas is still sitting near where he and Philip had played their game, on a rock a few feet from James, not far from the dirt path out of the clearing. He stares blankly at the others for a moment, then begins searching the ground around him. A smile lights his face as he reaches for a small, flat stone. Once again he begins to examine his fingernails. Finding one that needs attention, he touches the surface of the stone to it – and then stops. He looks over at Peter.

Peter has been sitting with his elbows on his thighs, hands loosely clasped before him, leaning forward, now and again shaking his head slightly. He has not been praying, but rather appears to be thinking things over, his eyes open, his features clouded. After a moment he meets Thomas's glance.

Still smiling, and without taking his eyes from Peter's, Thomas now applies the stone to his fingernail. The rasping sound attracts the attention of one or two of the others for a moment. Then they look away. Peter's expression is blank. After a few moments, while Thomas keeps on rasping away at his nail, Peter breaks their eye contact and looks off into the distance. He has betrayed no evidence of noticing what Thomas was doing. Thomas's face breaks into a grin as he now looks down and attends to a few more strokes on his nail. He stops, examines the nail, and feels it with his thumb. Then he drops the stone.

Andrew fidgets, biting a fingernail. "He *is* throwing himself away. He *is* destroying himself. Simon is right. He really is."

"How, Andrew?" Bartholomew asks. "How can the Son of God destroy himself?"

Andrew doesn't appear to have heard him. "He's been promising since the beginning to give himself up to the Romans to be killed, but we never understood or believed him. But, Son of God or not, he's . . . he's going to do it. One of us will actually hand him over. *Tonight*. Why? Why is he destroying himself?"

"Bartholomew, Andrew," says Peter. "What does it serve to dwell on such questions?"

"Peter," Philip snaps, "why are you trying to make them deny their fears?"

"Because he said tonight, 'Banish your fears.'"

Bartholomew is moving to and fro. "But *he* is the one who is frightening us, Peter, with the other words he spoke tonight. And the way he looks lately. His skin has gone yellow and clammy and flaccid, his face is gaunt; he breathes hard. His eyes burn as if with delirium – he acts almost . . . almost *possessed*. But he *does*, Peter!"

"He does," Andrew agrees. "It's true. We never spoke of it, but – did you notice the gleam in his eye the other day when he – when he killed the fig tree?" Andrew sets his jaw and gleams darkly; then he recoils, shuddering.

"Yes!" Bartholomew cries. "It was terrible. If he can bring the dead back to life, why couldn't he have brought forth fruit on that tree? He knew the season was late; look, none of the figs have borne fruit. Why did he have to kill it, when he found no fruit?"

"Good questions." Philip stands, his face hard as stone, pointing his finger as if with a sceptre at the fig tree just back of the center of the clearing. "*You shall never again bear fruit!* – and it withered away, just like that. And then he talked about hurling mountains into the sea through faith – as if we want to go around murdering trees and drowning mountains. That sounds more like Satan's work than God's."

"Philip!" Peter shouts.

Bartholomew whirls toward Peter, wringing his hands. "*But it does*, Peter! And all those terrible revelations on the Mount! Maybe he didn't talk to me about my liberation; I – I can't remember clearly any more. But do you remember how wild and fearsome he was then?"

"How could we forget?" Andrew asks. "Also: He has always warned and threatened the Pharisees, but these last few days he's cursed them!" He gestures viciously with a pointed finger. "Condemned them to damnation!"

Matthew's head is in his hands, his voice taut. "Why don't we stop talking about all that? I really don't want to think about it."

"But we *must*, Matthew," Philip says, "because

these are the truths of the moment!" His eyes flash as he imitates Jesus again. *"Alas for you, Pharisees and lawyers! Alas for you, hypocrites! Blind guides! Snakes! You viper's brood! Fools, fit for hell! Alas for you, you robbers, you liars, you murderers of the prophets! On you will fall the guilt for all the innocent blood spilt on the ground! Believe me, this generation will bear it all! How can you escape being condemned to hell?!"* –

"Stop it, stop it, stop it!" Bartholomew sinks to the dust, hands to his ears.

"But that's what he said," Philip rants, "and that's how he said it!"

From his rock, Peter thunders, *"Liar!* You speak his condemnations but omit the truths of their sins, which he told in detail!"

Philip gestures wildly. "All right, what about when he drove the traders out of the Temple? Wild-eyed, roaring that Scripture about robbers' caves over and over, turning their tables over on top of them! Do you know he broke one man's legs with his table and knocked him unconscious?"

"Are you sure?" Peter's eyes narrow.

"I certainly am! I stayed behind and tended him."

"That's the first I've heard of it."

"Because you didn't want to hear of it."

Peter pauses, looking at Philip. Then he says, quietly, "I believe you're lying, Philip. But never mind that. Tell me . . . what wellspring of venom are you trying to exhaust on us? Why must you continue to spit such gall at us? Haven't we all enough grief?"

Philip reflects for a moment.

"I'll tell you why, Peter. It's not venom. It's not gall. It's because it became clear to me long ago that none of us really has a shred of certainty or a scrap of hope to hold on to."

He takes a deep breath and exhales.

"I'll tell you the real reason I joined Jesus: because he offered hope and a promise of certainty. But I should have known better. Yes, I've become disillusioned – but who wants illusions? I don't. It did hurt for awhile, it's true. But now I realize it's a mistake for a man to stake his life on any promise of hope or certainty – except that of uncertainty itself. Uncertainty alone is certain. It's the only thing we can ever know. I see that now."

He moves over and takes a seat at the base of his tree, to the right of the clearing. "And now there's no more pain, Peter, and my eyes are clear, and I see people clinging frantically to shreds of mist and tatters of wind. Not 'spirit,' either. *Wind!* Empty, blowing air!

"The truth is, we can't agree on what he said or where, much less what he means by it. Each one of us sees, hears, touches, smells, and knows a different Jesus. Each one's Jesus is sometimes even antithetical to each other's Jesus.

"Look, we've seen mountainous waves calm instantly and storm clouds disappear; bodies turn to light or rise from death; loathesome, putrid diseases vanish like moonshadows moving into sunlight; *trees wither at a word!* And not only changes he appeared to effect – what of the ones that we did, or seemed to? Simply by saying a word, and blink! everything changes. And we've had no better idea what really happened than that fig tree did, the other day."

As Philip continues, several of the others unobtrusively cover or shield their ears.

"The truth is, the world is no longer reliable to us. And neither are our memories. Maybe he didn't knock that trader out the other day, maybe I didn't tend him. That's what I remember, but how do I know it's true? We've been arguing all night over what we believe we know as true, what we remember we knew as real. We guess, we imagine, we suppose; as 'brothers,' we try to agree, but we don't.

"How do we *know* he really is up on that hilltop now, or that this garden is really here, or that Judas isn't, or that we are – or that this is night, not day? How do we know?"

Bartholomew, in the dust, is almost in tears. "Please stop, Philip. *Please.*"

Philip doesn't move. "No," he says, firm and earnest. "You *listen.*" Then he shouts, "And Matthew! Andrew! *Uncover your ears!*"

Matthew, on his rock, grimly shakes his head. Andrew, sprawling on the ground, hesitates, then complies.

"Listen," Philip goes on. "As far as we can really see, the truth is that we all seem stuck in this idiot moment like slaves in a field. You're right, Peter. We can't get out. No way we can do anything but plow this field, row by row. The asses are dragging the plow, and the plow is dragging the asses. No way out till the field's all plowed. . . .

"No. No, even better, we're not the branches of the vine, as he said tonight; we're the fruit, the grapes themselves. We can't get off our own branches even if we want to. If the branches are bad, then the grapes are bad, and the whole thing gets lopped off and burnt."

Philip breaks a branch off a tree and throws it into the center of the clearing.

"But if the branches are good, then the grapes are good, and then what? Come harvest time, we're all picked and eaten, or thrown into vats and trampled to make wine." He stops, tilts his head. "Hm, listen to me. All of us. We're just like him now: Can't say anything, but we have to say it in donkeys, figs, or grapes.

"Well, anyway, *either way*, bad grapes or good, there's no way out till 'what must happen has happened,' right, Jesus? Till we're all dead, in other words. Till nothing survives of us but distorted images in other men's memories."

He pauses to survey the others, pursing his lips. Peter is listening.

"But instead of accepting that," Philip goes on, "we

all cling to his pretty promises as security. 'The Kingdom of Heaven': a star that seems to shine until you look closely: then it's gone. 'Eternal life.' Froth. Eternal death! One moment he plays on our fears of Satan and damnation, and the next on our dreams of a paradise to come.

"The Scriptures also promise all that and attribute the promises to God, of course, but how do we know they – and he – weren't dreamt up themselves? There hasn't been a legitimate prophet in the Land in five hundred years. How do we know there ever was?

"Now: Do we face that, and accept it? No. We cling all the more frantically to shreds of mist, to tatters of wind.

"Well, I am going to cut away our grips, Peter, even if I have to cut away our fingers. Because I know from experience we'll all be better off, better off facing and living with uncertainty and hopelessness."

Peter remains calm. "You've never said anything like that before, Philip. You who've called him Master and Lord."

"Because you never wanted to hear it, and I am no fool. But now you have to hear it, and so must they all."

"Looking after them, eh, like James Alphaeus?" Peter looks at Philip more closely. "That's not why you're so poisonously bitter, Philip. You wouldn't be that way. You'd be a much more compassionate man.

"No. You're drowning us in your bile because you're afraid, Philip. Not of Satan and damnation. You don't really accept that, either."

Peter stops, his eyes narrowing as he gazes at Philip. Then his face relaxes, and his tone of voice softens.

"No, Philip, you're afraid of something quite different from all that. You're afraid that we have good reason to hope, despite uncertainty. You're afraid that it takes more courage to have faith than to resign oneself to hopelessness. You're afraid to risk yourself on the chance there might be unimaginably fine cloth and leather beneath those shreds of promises.

"And what's even worse to you in some ways, you can't bear the thought that you might be alone, and wrong. You're too vain and fearful, Philip, to face your own honest fear. To acknowledge it like the fool that you are, that we all are. To confess it and be just like everybody else.

"But the honesty of your fear, Philip – and the honesty and depth of your love of him – that's why *you* haven't left. That's why you're still here."

"That's nonsense," Philip says.

"Maybe – but it's the truth." Peter pauses. "And if you don't admit it, then . . . *you're* a hypocrite, yourself."

Philip does not reply but does not lower his eyes or turn from Peter's gaze.

Bartholomew is still sitting in the dust. "But Peter, maybe he's right. You can't deny Jesus has become wild and fearsome, ranting and cursing. Killing a tree because it had no fruit to feed him, Peter? The Prophet of Love? The Source of Eternal Life? With his ribs poking through his skin, and his skin . . . smelling as if it were decaying on his bones, and his face contorted in a curse, and his eyes burning and scorching us all?

"And what *about* those swords? Does he mean for us to become killers? *Murderers?!*" He shivers and sucks his breath in through his teeth. "Maybe Philip is right. And James too. Doesn't he seem terribly changed and strange to you now, Peter?"

Peter hasn't moved from his rock in a long while. Now he sighs, rises heavily, and takes a slow step or two. He looks down at his clasped and wringing hands. "Yes. He does. I won't deny it. I don't mind the curses – as the Father's true Son, he must be terrible in rage as well as graceful in love. And he was *healing people* all the way to Jerusalem, remember . . . but . . . he seems to have lost his strength. Tonight, even when he spoke of love, he sat so small and still, his words like hollow whispers, as if he were hardly even there."

Peter sighs, and shakes his head once, then twice. "I – I can't look at his face now, without having to turn away. I don't understand what he's doing any more than the rest of you.

"In a way, I'm like Simon. I too seek fulfillment in this life, here and now. I've been waiting all along for him to initiate the real work and my real service – the founding and organizing of his Church! That is his own true and avowed mission, Simon. So I have been straining at the bit for action, too. But he has only continued preaching and healing and proclaiming his Gospel all over the countryside, winning more and more followers. I can see that the Church must be built upon his love, and no one can spread that better than he – but, still. . . .

"And now he's come to Jerusalem, to kill and to be – killed . . . himself. No doubt he will be. All the authorities thirst for his blood now. He says it has to happen so that we may receive the Spirit and so that he may rise again, conquering death. I don't really know what that means any more than the rest of you. I don't understand the swords. Maybe he means to test us, even as the Father tested Abraham, commanding him to kill his only-begotten son. Eh, James? No . . . that makes no sense. I, too, am confused."

Peter looks up and around at the others, and force returns to his words. "But brothers, I can't question him. I've seen his miracles, I've heard his wisdom, I've felt his love working within me deeper than my mind, memory, or senses could ever penetrate. Who can fathom his will? All I can do is follow blindly, and hope, and wait. All I can do is give myself to him." He sits again.

Andrew's eyes are shining. "Yes! We must only give ourselves to him! Remember, he gave us promises tonight of love and joy, of completing our joy. He *will* send the Spirit soon after him. He *will* come to us again in the coming age. We shall be judges sitting by his side in Heaven, in the constant presence of the Father. Bartholomew, he prayed to the Father tonight; he's given everything to the Father! Not to himself! . . . And then we shall know everything. He promised just tonight!"

Bartholomew's voice is broken. "But maybe his promises are 'shreds of mist.' He made promises and prayed after the Seder, but now he's gone up to the hill-top to weep and wail and cry. Maybe he doesn't believe those promises himself."

"Don't say that!" Matthew claps his hands to his ears again, and spits his words out one at a time, as if unable to hold them back. "If his words are not true, then he is not the Messiah – and he's damned . . . and we're all lost – and abandoned – and damned ourselves." He lets out a cry. "Master, let it not be so! *Please*, Lord!"

Andrew looks at him wide-eyed, and speaks in a soothing tone. "Don't you have faith in him, Matthew? Bartholomew? I know you love him, surely you believe him. I love him, I believe him. He *has to* speak the truth. He's the Son of God!"

"Andrew . . . " Peter frowns, a hand on his belly. "I agree with what you say about him; but I'm very weary, and my bowels are just as troubled as anyone else's . . . and I can no longer bear your lies, brother."

"What do you mean, Peter?" Andrew asks, sincerely. "You're not making any sense."

"Your words are right, but they don't come from a pure heart. I can tell when you're faking, brother. You've been trying for a long time to convince yourself that you love Jesus and have faith in him, but you're lying to yourself and us all, even now. You don't keep his commandments, and you don't love him."

Tears come to Andrew's eyes. "Why do you turn against me, Peter? He told us of the two main Commandments tonight; I try to keep them. I love God with my all. I love my neighbor as much as myself." He speaks firmly. "I know I do."

Andrew pauses. The tears are rolling down his cheeks. "*I do!* But – and I even love Jesus far more; I love him as much as I love myself! And almost as much as I love God! But" – he tries to compose himself – "I don't see why he gives these as commandments – and he doesn't mention faith in him in *them* – but in the next moment he insists that unless we have complete faith in him, we are doomed. Not that I don't have that faith; I just don't understand."

"Because the Father is working only through His Son." Peter is tiring. "You sound unsure of yourself, Andrew. Do you really have all this faith and love you claim?"

"I wouldn't claim them at all, if you weren't prying into me! Maybe you're questioning me because *you* don't have love and faith! Maybe you're jealous of me, Peter."

"What nonsense. You talk a lot, but I don't see much in your actions to indicate such boundless love – "

"Who was the one to comfort Thaddeus when you were busy threatening him? *Me*, not you! You confine yourself to noble talk and parables."

"Listen to you. You probably have all your good acts chalked up on a little mental slate, eh? Some real comfort you gave him, if that's what you were thinking of when you did it. You're as vain as a cock! You don't know what love is."

"And you *do?*" Andrew's voice is shrill. "And faith also? You who are going to deny him *three times* before the cock crows? Some faith you must have. Some love. Yes, indeed, the Rock of the Church!"

Peter strikes at his own heart. "He is *my Lord!* I said I would die with him. I *will* die with him! You shut your mouth!"

"Why should that bother you, Simon Peter? You're the Rock, aren't you? Brothers, look, the Rock is cracking! What shall we do – what, indeed, shall we do?"

"You jealous little hypocrite! I told you to *shut your mouth!*"

Peter lunges at Andrew to strike him, but Andrew, who's been sitting near the large end of the great boulder, dashes behind it and around. Peter wheels back toward the center of the clearing to run for him but is caught by Simon and Philip, who restrain him. He flings them away and goes to stand near his seat, brooding and furious.

Philip looks at Peter, then Andrew, then James, then John.

"If this is what being brothers is about," he says,

in low tones, "maybe we'd better pass it up." He leans against a tree.

"Oh, everything is going so bad," Bartholomew laments. "How can they be so spiteful? . . . and him – so . . . cruel." He shakes his head. "The *Messiah?!* How – ?" A gleam shines forth in his eyes, as he wonders. "Maybe that's why he's so terrible now, and sickly. He's up there crying – maybe he's . . . *fallen*. Maybe he's begging forgiveness! Maybe *that's why* he's going to be betrayed and killed!"

Bartholomew lurches to his feet and looks at the others in horror and confusion. Peter is praying fervently. Some of the others glance back, but none speak. Bartholomew continues muttering, half to himself, half to others. "Won't someone say something? You're all mute as trees. Silent as stones! . . . Could it be – *not* the Christ?! Essenes – two Messiahs. Pharisees – no Messiahs. Wonder – what the stars . . . foretell. Persians? . . . I don't know. Others claim to be! He says there'll be false ones" – he stops in mid-step, one foot in the air – "maybe: maybe *he* is!"

Bartholomew stares, pursing his lips. He becomes lucid for a few moments, except that he's still standing with one foot in the air. "Maybe he *is* the Devil! If the Devil could show him all the world in a vision, couldn't the Devil be responsible for all those miracles and healings? Maybe he's an Evil Shepherd, planning to devour us! Maybe he *is* the Prince of Devils!

"Could we be following Satan, all these years?" He puts his other foot down. "Doing the Devil's work and not God's? Now . . . *murderers?*" He reels against a tree and closes his eyes, then speaks in less than a whisper. "Oh, Lord! God of Abraham! Do You hear me? Are you here, Lord? Do I still stand in Your presence? If I have been following Satan, Father, please forgive me. Please don't condemn me to darkness. I only wanted to live in Your Light, Father! I only wanted You, Father! Have *mercy on me*, oh my God!"

Bartholomew falls to the ground and sobs for a moment. Suddenly he sits up, staring, and begins to rant. "The *rest – all –* so many thousands! All he does is heal . . . they think he's the Christ! What if – . . . *all* . . . damnation . . . *darkness –* for his own glory?! Said his message would spread to all nations – maybe he really *accepted* the Devil's offer! Said he's conquered the world – planning? to lead it to *damnation?* And then God will *have to destroy it!* No choice! Maybe that's what he means: *the end of time!*"

Peter bolts upright. "Bartholomew, shut your vile blasphemous mouth! Now *listen!*"

All listen. Not a sound can be heard.

"He's . . . our Master's weeping again." Peter pauses, listens, then lays his head in his hands. "While we're down here becoming demons, Jesus, our Lord, is up there weeping. Our Christ is crying to God!"

Peter, Thomas, Andrew, and Matthew begin to cry.

The others stare in shock or exhaustion. James Alphaeus sobs a prayer: "Jesus? Master, please don't make the world end! Don't lead us into *damnation*, Lord Jesus! Forgive us our trespasses! Thine is the Kingdom! We aren't trespassing in your Kingdom, Lord! It's *yours!*" He wails, becoming frantic. "You're the *Good Shepherd*, Lord! We won't betray you! We won't! Please don't curse us, Lord! We're good sheep! Don't kill us! We're good trees – we'll bear fruit!

"Please don't send me to the fires, Lord! I'll burn! I'll die! Come down, Good Shepherd! Come down from the hill! Please don't curse me. I'm a good – sheep! Please . . . "

He collapses in tears and gasping sobs. Thomas, still sobbing himself, goes over to him and puts an arm around his shoulder.

Bartholomew is walking as if in a trance and speaking in an eerie singsong.

"Cry and weep. Shepherd and sheep. Don't cry, Shepherd! Don't weep, sheep! Up there, down here; what difference? Everybody crying. Why? Did *he* hear me blaspheming? *He heard!* He knows! He's *here*, right *now* – he's *present!* He's presence! He said he's in the Father, and the Father's in the present, the Father knows, the Father's here, so – *he heard!*

"The herd! He's the herd! And the herdsman, too? And here in my heart as well? He said so! Just tonight! 'I am in you, and you in me.' Can it be so? And we're all in the Father? And the Father's in us all? What's in? Where's

154

out? The whole Kingdom? Herdsman and herd! Shepherd and sheep!"

Peter has been listening again. Now, desolate, he says, "Still crying . . . you're still weeping . . . oh Master. Still weeping."

"Crying. To the Father!" Bartholomew is hoarse. "For *forgiveness!* . . . *Evil*, evil, evil, evil! 'No one is good but God alone' – *he* admitted that. A lamb *couldn't* be a Good Shepherd . . . but – a *lion* – evil! Planning to devour us! To roast us in the fires!" He stops and grasps at his chest. "But he's *in my heart!* I can't get him out!"

Bartholomew looks at some of the others with a vacant gaze, then wobbles and slowly spins around in the clearing, still muttering. "Philip's right . . . just asses plowing a row – like this ant crawling up my leg." He drops to one knee. "End of the row – kneecap – thwack! God kills us. Evil Shepherd . . . from within. Evil Shepherd kills us with a sword from within. God wants us dead. Eat us grapes, drink us wine – roast us lambs!" He speaks to the ant, "Have faith!" and then strikes it with a fingernail.

Simon has been looking on in confusion; now he grins. "Wait! That's murder! Capital crime! A sin! 'An eye for an eye.' I'm afraid we'll have to arrange an immediate tribunal and execution!

"Why trouble yourself?" Bartholomew asks, numbly. "I'll be disposed of at the end of time, which could happen any moment now."

Thaddeus has also been looking on with dull eyes for a long time. Now he smiles, glancing at Simon. "No – it's the cross for you!"

Simon and Thaddeus leap up and grab Bartholomew, each holding out an arm and lifting him under the shoulder. Bartholomew's eyes go white, and he sags like a sack. Simon and Thaddeus support him while looking around.

"No crosses here," Simon mumbles. "Guess we'll have to nail him up to that fig" – he nods at the one just beyond the center of the clearing. "Nail him up to the Tree of Life!"

They begin to drag Bartholomew to the tree, but before they can take three steps, Philip leaps in front of them, his words like knives. "For God's sake, put him down and stop this insane play! Can't you see he's on the verge of going mad? You idiots!"

Simon and Thaddeus look at Bartholomew, place him on a rock, and return to their own, embarrassed. Philip continues. "Now, Bartholomew, enough of your babbling. And the rest of you can stop blubbering. Your Master has ceased his weeping."

"Yes," James says, "I think he has."

No one speaks for awhile as the others compose themselves. Philip and James, who has been watching and listening without moving, glance bleakly at one another.

James speaks first. "We always have been under

the grindstone to one extent or another."

"But never like this." Philip frowns, prodding his belly. "God, never like this."

"And I suppose you're right. We can't get out from under till we've been ground to fine flour, I guess."

"You know one thing that galls me?" A pained grin plays on Philip's face. "Bartholomew reminded me of it during his ravings. It amazes me, too, because they've seen him humiliating us all along! I mean how everyone is always saying, 'Oh, how blessed you are to be an Apostle of the Christ. It must be such a wonderful life!' I've never had the energy in one of those moments to tell someone what it's *really* like, being with him. 'I met him once, and he cured my goiter, so he must keep you in ecstasy all the time.' Roses and rainbows forever, they think."

James fingers a bush. "But roses have thorns, and rainbows appear only after storms, eh?"

"If at all."

"Mm . . . say, speaking of Bartholomew, do you think maybe he was having a vision or a revelation? No, I'm serious. Maybe he received the Spirit. Maybe he had an illumination."

Philip can barely contain his laughter. "Bartholomew? That's no prophet foaming with vision, that's a frightened man on the verge of lunacy. It only sounded visionary because he can recite the entire Oriental gospel, all the revelations of Jesus, the complete

157

Apocrypha, and the Essene manuscripts word for word, as well as the secret techniques of Egyptian mummy makers and all the mystical astrological froth of every precinct of the heavens at any given moment – but he doesn't *know* a damned thing. He never has, and he doesn't now. All that stuff just scrambled in his head, and out it came. Bartholomew doesn't have any better an idea what 'Spirit' is than you do, James.

"I mean, all of us have seen remarkable things around Jesus, even Pharisees like Nicodemus. But what use are phantom visions in this moment? They can't strike much root in the soil of a garden like this. This is no Eden, in case you haven't noticed."

Peter rouses himself. "Even after all this, you two still choose to talk rather than to pray? Even now?"

Philip shrugs and goes to sit with Bartholomew. Some of the others are praying. Some are just sitting very still, exhausted.

"Peter," James says, "maybe my way of praying *is* with words. Maybe talking *is* praying, for me."

"What kind of nonsense is that?" Peter closes his eyes, takes a deep breath, and lets it out slowly. "James, as long as you keep up this idle questioning and doubting and wondering and talking, you are leaving yourself open to Satan. And one day he'll have you for good, like he does the Master's betrayer. Who may indeed be any one of us – I've never heard such evil talk."

James looks up to the skies, shaking his head. "Will

you consider what I'm saying for a moment? I'm talking to a wall. . . . Listen, Peter: if my way of praying leaves me open to Satan, I'll have to risk it. I can't accept that he'll ever have anyone forever, even the betrayer. I still feel that if I keep turning my soul to the Lord my God, He will always redeem me, He will lead me to the light of truth and salvation. But clearly you believe I'm in danger of casting myself into the everlasting pit at this very moment – so won't you even extend a hand to rescue me?"

"*I* cannot rescue you, brother. The Father has given all authority to him; and he does only as the Father bids him. Only *he* can redeem you – but not if you don't listen to what he says and put faith in it. The redemption he promises is nothing momentary, always needing to be renewed again and again. It is eternal salvation: baptism in the Holy Spirit, the Light of truth itself. Yet you test his every word like a Pharisee."

"Look, Peter." James is staring off into space as ideas come to him. "Don't you agree that anything he does, or anything the Father does through him, must be good, though we may not see it so or understand it?"

Peter sighs. "Yes. Of course."

"So that means that, because the Pharisees and his betrayer and, for that matter, hell itself, and the Prince of Evil, and lust, and hypocrisy, and all other sins, all these things exist in the world – so they must have been created by the Father through him – so therefore they must all be *good*. Not on the surface; but at its core, what can ultimately be bad, or evil? If he has made and is in them all, how can they be irredeemable?"

Peter doesn't hesitate. "Because, as you would say, they have turned away from his face; because through evil they have cut themselves off from him. Now they have no core. They are empty."

He glares at James, taking a long breath. "But how can you even ask that question when he has *said* that he condemns them? The fact that we find his teachings self-contradictory, James, only shows how limited our minds are in themselves. Philip's right, at least on that point. What can we know of truth, of Spirit, with our minds? If intellect were the gate to the Kingdom of Heaven, and logic were the steps to the throne, do you not think the lawyers would now be exalted on high? Instead they are damned! He has said so!

"And as long as we are reciting his words, *he said*, 'For as the Father has life-giving power in himself, so has the Son, by the Father's gift. As Son of Man, he has also been given the right to pass judgment. *Do not wonder at this*, because the time is coming when all who are in the grave shall hear his voice and come out: those who have done right will rise to life; those who have done wrong will rise to hear their doom.' He said that in Jerusalem one Sabbath day, remember?"

James nods.

"Then what more is there to be said now?"

James sighs, and shifts on his rock. "I don't know. I keep thinking of what Simon said awhile ago: If He had wanted me different, He would have made me so. Does the Lord God, terrible but full of grace, create beings just to throw them away to doom?"

He doesn't allow Peter to reply. "Listen, Peter. You remember earlier, when we were playing and throwing his sayings around and around. Not you – I mean some of us. Well, that was no game for me – that's the way my mind works every waking moment. Even in my dreams, too! I can't stop it. I have to give myself up to it. To turn those paradoxical sayings over and over, to grind them against one another like uncut stones, to look through them at myself and the world and see if I get a clear image.

"And I do, often; I'm not as ignorant as I made out earlier, that was just to make a point. I feel if I can just devote myself to this mental work completely, sooner or later the gem of truth must shine forth. It must!

"But I admit" – James ponders for a moment – "yes, I see now, that I was in a sense using the Law as a shield between me and Jesus's words. Instead I should cast myself into the whirlwind between the two, perhaps – and if I do, I will surely lose my footing. And that means being uncertain. So for me it does take courage to choose uncertainty, Peter. But I must throw myself into the Master's words, if I am to be his disciple. I must seek truth in his revelation. That is clear."

Peter slaps his palm against the rock. "But James, our work has nothing to do with constant puzzling over his words! He says we are only to receive his commands and *obey* them, to receive his words and *act* upon them."

"Peter!" James shouts as loud as he can. "I *am* receiving his words and acting upon them!" He quiets himself. "Not in the same way as you, but that's *your* work. I'm not obeying his commands, exactly – but maybe he intends that statement just to add urgency to my work, by extending the paradox to include a contradiction between my nature and his commands. . . . I don't know. Maybe I'm all confused.

"I'll tell you this, though, to anticipate your next point: it's only by considering his words and looking through them at myself and others that I've come to know anything at all of love. You and the others think I have no heart at all, but I do, and it's not barren. I can't express the love I feel, but it's there. And it has grown only through my growth in understanding."

Peter is looking off into the distance, shaking his head in short, sharp motions. James continues. "I haven't memorized his every word, like you, Peter, but I have listened to him, and I've suffered, too. All the times he's reproached us, often with an extra glance at me, for not knowing what he meant. Continual shudders of self-recognition during his accusations against the lawyers and scribes. Days of trying to stop asking or even thinking of questions. Secretly wondering, Peter, if I must become like *you* to enter the Kingdom of Heaven. Finally saying to myself, I cannot change my own nature.

"Listen, everyone must have a specific task he's called for, Peter; different ones, especially among the Twelve. Are the twelve tribes of Israel the same, or the twelve houses of the stars? No indeed. Would you seek to change them?"

"I seek to change no one and no thing," Peter says. "I only ask you to have faith in him and his words."

"Peter, I think I can devote myself to total absorption in his words – but I can't believe in him as Messiah until I know it." James speaks with force. "He has said the pupil must reach the stature of his teacher. When I have attained to his stature, then I will know."

"That makes no sense to me." Peter exhales. "After all those miracles? After he bestowed healing power on us all, and the power to cast out devils? How could he possibly do that if he weren't the Son of God?"

"What about what Bartholomew said, about power coming from the Devil?"

"You, a man of reason, listening to the rantings of a man half-possessed?" Peter sighs. "James, you're wearing me out."

"All right," James says, "but who can be consistent at a time like this?" He stops, cocks his head, thinking. "Look at it another way. You would say the way those powers worked was, we said the name and if the person had faith, he became whole; if not, he didn't. But none of us know what forces actually worked in what ways upon what sicknesses or demons. Philip *is* right; to this day, I haven't quite been able to accept the evidence of my senses, with those healings. Yet there's no doubt they happened.

"So my question is this. If God can cause these cures to happen with power moving through ignorant fools like us, what's to say Jesus isn't equally ignorant of the real processes at work? Maybe God has given more power to Jesus's name than he's given to Jesus himself. Maybe He just gives him hints, and Jesus is always playing the situation. That would explain his slips, like the one Thomas saw. Jesus himself says he's just a medium for the Father's will, doing only what the Father wants and saying only the Father's words."

"And you accept that?" Peter asks.

"Yes."

"Then you must believe him when he says that he is the Messiah, the Christ, the Son of God! There, James. You're trapped in your own logic!" Peter's face is drawn, and there is no trace of victory in his eyes or his words.

James struggles to reply. "Wait a moment. He never explicitly said all that. And what does it mean anyway? 'Christ.' 'Messiah.' 'Anointed.'" He shrugs. "He only hints, Peter, he makes allusions. And he calls himself the 'Son of Man.'"

"James, don't evade me." Peter's anger rises.

"Admit that you stepped into your own trap!"

"Peter," Andrew says quietly, "I think what James is saying is that we've all had so much evasive and ambiguous language" –

"You stay out of it!" Peter snaps. "'Evasive language' – how can you *possibly* – " Peter glares at Andrew, shaking his head, and then turns back toward James.

"James, do you remember in Caesarea Philippi when he asked, 'Who do they say I, the Son of Man, am?' And we told him and he asked, 'Who do *you* say I am?' And I said, 'You are the Messiah!' What did he say then? James?"

Silence.

"Tell me!"

James is looking down. "He said you learned that from no man, but it was revealed to you by God Himself, and that you will be the Rock of his Church."

"Precisely!" Peter shouts. "Now that was even more direct, and more powerful, than saying, 'I am the Messiah.' And then he ordered us not to tell anyone who he is.

"If you don't believe that *that* is explicit, James, you'd better begin to face your own self-deception. That's all I have to say."

James has no reply, but Thomas cuts in, speaking from James Alphaeus's side with a hand still on his shoulder. "Listen, Peter, you may be right about what Jesus says, but spare us what you 'have to say,' if you don't mind. Jesus himself may have been wondering then what or who he is, and may have felt so pleased with your reply that he decided to herd us all into believing it! Did you in fact experience that as a revelation from God, or did you just say it to please him? Hah! I can see your answer in your eyes."

Thomas pauses, then tilts his head, grinning. "And in fact, if I recall, not too long after you blurted that out, he began telling us what would happen here in Jerusalem 'these very days.' And you, in all your glory, said to him, 'Heaven forbid! This will never happen to you, Lord!' What did he say then, Rock?"

Peter, jaws set, looks away.

"You *are* a rock! You have obsidian jaws and eyes of stone, Rock! You and your basalt biceps! Hah! I'll tell you what he said then: '*Get thee behind me, Satan; you are a stumbling-block to me!*'

"He stubs his toe on you, you boulder! You pebble! *He's* the cornerstone, and they'll reject him – but you're a *pebble*, to be stumbled upon and kicked aside! He said that you think as men think, not as God thinks! So if you please, Simon Peter, *spare us your high and mighty thoughts!*"

James, Philip, and Andrew nod in agreement, aroused at Peter. Some of the others look on without moving, as if deaf; some sleep, utterly spent.

Peter sits in stillness for a long time. His face softens as he thinks. Then he speaks again, without looking up at first.

"You are right. My thoughts are worthless, they are the thoughts of a blind intellect.

"And so for all our thoughts, brothers. Yes – the word 'brother' is alien to us at this moment – that is the devilish power of our thoughts. They puff us up, divide us like these shadows, make us vain and vengeful against one another. Despite moments of brotherhood and love – given to us through his grace – moments when we knew we were one, when we swore we would always stand by one another, no matter what.

"Is there room, brothers, for doubtful and questioning thoughts in love? Is there, John? We do not love each other, we doubt and question each other. We do not love our Lord and Master, we doubt and question him. These are the acts of selves protecting themselves. But in love the self willingly strips itself of all protection. It gives itself away, it throws itself to a certain death. A death as inevitable, and painful, and slow as a crucifixion. 'Lay down your self, pick up your cross' – that's what he requires of his followers, of us.

"Yet all he requires, truly, is that we truly love God and man and truly love and have faith in him. And there is no real difference between loving the Father and loving him; as he told Philip, having seen him, we have seen the Father – and so it is with love and faith. And if the Father and Son are in us all, let us love Them in each other. The Father loves us so much He has given us His son to save us. And Jesus has always loved us; but we have all betrayed his love and his faith. Now we are already scattered, even as he promised.

"If we love him, we must have faith in him. If we have faith, then we must love him. And what is it to love him? 'To receive my commands and obey them'; that is all. He said it tonight.

"*Brothers!*" Some of the sleepers start, and awaken. "Who are *we* to question him? What is our intellect before his wisdom, before his power and grace? Give up this pretentious intellect and self, lay them down at his feet. Pray to him, beseech him, cry to him for faith. Surely he will give it to you. He has said, 'Ask and you will receive.' 'Blessed are they who mourn, they shall receive consolation.' Mourn your own fickle and way-ward soul, mourn your own lack of faith – surely he will console you. Can he possibly seek to deceive us, to offer us an empty word?

"So let us give ourselves up to him. Let us bow our heads, attach our minds to his heart, cling to his feet with such a grip of strength and utter abandon that we become as a part of him. When he moves, we move; when he stays, we stay; where he lives, we live, and there is no trace of our selves elsewhere. This is the way of faith, brothers, and you know this is the way he wants us to follow.

"What if sometimes he drags us over deserts and rocky ground? You cannot expect eternal gardens in this world – not now, anyway. What if he does require us to kill in his name, to murder? Have such faith that even were he to drag you into the pits of hell and abandon you there, you would still think only of him in your heart, believing fully that he is your Lord and Savior, and that he will rescue you from perdition and grant you eternal life, when the right hour for you arrives. Thomas – Philip – James: You *must* have faith! And give up this Satanic questioning or – I know it in my heart – you will be bound to take a terrible fall.

"Has such a one as he ever walked this earth before? If you still have strength to think, think about that. Brothers, you and I – we, his Twelve chosen ones, chosen to be Apostles of his mission in this world and judges in the world to come over the twelve tribes of Israel, which were chosen by the Father Himself – we, brothers, have been witness to the might and grace of the Lord Jesus Christ from the very beginning. We have seen masses cured of all ills just by his presence, James; without a word or anything else except their faith and his Messianic power! We have seen the fiercest and most terrible devils thrown out at his command. And it is something to wonder at, that even these most loathesome, darkest spirits in the creation instantly recognize him as the Anointed One, the Son of God; but we, who have been granted his most glorious blessings on no account of our own, we who by his unfathomable grace have been selected out of all the children of Israel to be his closest and dearest servants – *we* are the ones who still persist in questioning him, in doubting him. Even though we have seen with our own eyes the prophet Elijah and the mighty giver of God's Law, Moses, standing in humble attendance upon him; even though we have witnessed the Heavens open and heard with our own ears the terrible voice of the Almighty Father saying of him, *'This is My Son, My Most Beloved'?!*

"Brothers! How can we do this? From what stinking pit in our hearts can we dredge up the audacity to entertain even for an instant the thought that he is not our Messiah? When we have seen him transfigured into pure Light, before which our mighty sun appeared to be a mere moon and all the things of this world paled like forgotten dreams and we fell on our faces in wonder and awe? When he has been confirmed as Messiah before us – and us *alone* – by the greatest souls of all time, and blessed by God Himself?

"And now we sit here and bicker like lawyers while he is off praying to his Father with all his might. Better we should rip off our clothes, prostrate in this cold dust, and cry and wail to God for forgiveness and mercy. Because the hour, the very moment of his betrayal has already come – in every single mind and heart and soul in this garden tonight, it has come. What happens next can only bring our inner deeds to the sordid light of day. John speaks the truth: How bad can the fires and pits of hell be, for souls such as ours right now? Loveless, faithless, burning with spite, feeding on deceit even as earthworms feed on earth. Were it not for his grace which he has promised us, we should instantly clothe ourselves in sackcloth and ashes and mourn the damnation of our own souls – for I promise you, they would be eternally damned. No wonder he went apart from us to pray, to weep and cry before his Father, for our forgiveness. No wonder he has to die for our sins. No wonder."

Some of the others have fallen asleep again. One or two have turned away. The rest sit listening, with heads bowed.

Thomas says, quietly, "Three times, Peter."

Peter has not moved from his seat during his entire speech. Now, head in hands, he does not respond.

There is only silence. After a while, a little movement; they are all falling asleep. The breezes of the evening have died away, but a chill has settled upon them. Some try to huddle more tightly under their cloaks, shivering in their sleep.

At last only James is awake, but his head is nodding.

Finally he too yields to slumber.

Apparently the moon has gone down, for the garden is steeped in darkness and silence.

END

Afterword

Upon finishing the first draft of *While Jesus Weeps,* now more than twenty-five years ago, I knew it was a unique presentation of the story of Jesus of Nazareth. However others may perceive it, I received it as "given" inspiration. It was a divine blessing that evoked wonder and gratitude in me and taught me many things.

For a number of personal and spiritual reasons, I have kept the manuscript on a shelf all these years.

Now the time has come to release it.

I first wrote *While Jesus Weeps* as a play, and only transposed it into narrative form a few years ago. Even so, in essence and in all substantial details the book you have before you is still the same one I wrote in 1971-72.

In my research I relied almost entirely on the New English translation of the canonical Gospels of Matthew, Mark, Luke, and John. On occasion, when quoting famous passages, I have used the better known King James versions of these four standard Gospels. I have not drawn on any of the ensuing portions of the *New Testament.* Nor have I drawn on material from the Nag Hammadi scrolls, or on any of the apocryphal legends of Jesus's life.

It was a matter of spiritual principle to proceed this way. I felt obliged to conform this rendition of these crucial events entirely to the Gospel canon. *While Jesus Weeps* had to be fundamentally consistent with the essence of the Jesus story as it has been honored by

Christians and others the world over for nearly two thousand years. I am aware of the modern critical "quest for the historical Jesus," and was from the beginning of my work on this book. But such matters did not concern me. Whatever may or may not have actually happened two millenia ago in Palestine, I knew that nothing in this story could diverge in any essential way from the "gospel truths" as told in the *New Testament* – even if, as is sometimes the case, those "truths" contradict one another from one Gospel to the next.

All that being said, by necessity this whole story is an exercise in poetic license. In the canonical Gospels, we learn very little about the Apostles. Even their leaders, such as Peter and John ("the Beloved"), are only minimally rendered. And we have no detail in any of the Gospels that suggests what might have transpired among the Apostles in Gethsemane. All we are told is that they fell asleep twice and were awakened both times by Jesus! *While Jesus Weeps* is therefore an almost entirely imaginary presentation. And, of course, it is only one among limitless ways that we might conceive what happened among those men that night.

This is thus a story of the dark night of the soul, here shown vis-a-vis the traditional Christian legend and message. Without descent into and broken-hearted passage through a Gethsemane of the soul as imagined here, no deep self-knowledge awakens. Without such self-awareness, no true Pentecost, or fully transformative baptism by the living divine Spirit, can be received. Thus I have been taught, and thus I have understood by direct realization and in my own sacred work with others.

To my view, such passages provide the medicine our souls most require for ultimate growth in Spirit. Only thus can we purify from millennia of idealistic abstractions about the work of spiritual salvation and emancipation. Only thus can we even begin to comprehend the nature, character, and work of our divine teachers. And, I believe, only thus can we find out what it takes for us to complete our discipleships – and to stand forth, ourselves, as authentic "sons and daughters of God."

About the Author

Born in New York in 1950, Saniel Bonder grew up in a Jewish family in a small, mostly Christian town in the southern U. S. He has dedicated his entire adult life to personal growth, sacred transformation, and, beginning in 1993, spiritual teaching. He lives in northern California and is learning the art of the *bansuri,* the classical North Indian bamboo flute.

For information on Saniel's other publications and his sacred work, please contact Mt. Tam Awakenings:

Phone: toll-free 888-741-5000
Fax: 415-721-0111
Web site: www.sanielbonder.com
E-mail: info@sanielbonder.com